# The Mediterranean Diet Cookbook

# The Mediterranean Diet Cookbook

**DR CATHERINE ITSIOPOULOS** (PhD APD)

MACMILLAN
Pan Macmillan Australia

First published 2015 in Macmillan by Pan Macmillan Australia Pty Ltd
1 Market Street, Sydney, New South Wales, Australia, 2000

Photography by John Laurie
Additional photography by Jeremy Simons and Shutterstock
Styling by Caroline Velik
Additional styling by Bernadette Smithies
Editing by Samantha Sainsbury and Nicola Young
Design and layout by Debra Billson
Series design by Trisha Garner
Additional typesetting by Post Pre-press
Illustrations by Shutterstock
Index by Puddingburn
Colour and reproduction by Splitting Image

Cataloguing-in-Publication entry is available
from the National Library of Australia
http://catalogue.nla.gov.au

The author and the publisher have made every effort to contact copyright
holders for material used in this book. Any person or organisation that
may have been overlooked should contact the publisher.

10 9 8 7 6 5 4 3 2

Dedicated to my husband Savvas Koutsis, who has inspired
me to appreciate the art and pleasure of food.

To my darling daughters Tiana and Vivienne Koutsis,
your love of food has been my motivation for this second book.
May you create your own special food memories and
continue to pass them on.

To my mother, Theano, mother-in-law, Paraskevi and the mothers
of my dear friends, your recipes will continue to bring us joy
for generations to come.

# Contents

## PART TWO
### *Traditional Mediterranean Recipes*

# Introduction

The Mediterranean diet has been a healthy traditional lifestyle across the olive-growing areas of the Mediterranean for thousands of years. It's not a 'diet' in the sense of restricting food intake to achieve weight loss. On the contrary, it's a one-size-fits-all healthy way of eating that focuses on what you *can* eat rather than what you can't. It's a tasty cuisine based on enjoyment of fresh ingredients from the land and the sea, sourced from local gardens and markets, carefully prepared with love, and enjoyed – often with a glass of homemade wine – with friends and family.

The Mediterranean diet is the most comprehensively researched and scientifically validated diet in the world. Studies have repeatedly shown it to be the ideal diet for maintaining a healthy heart, as well as preventing diabetes and metabolic syndrome (including fatty liver, abdominal obesity and insulin resistance), some cancers, Alzheimer's disease and Parkinson's disease. It may even help prevent depression. Recent studies have also shown that it may promote longevity by protecting DNA.

## ABOUT THIS BOOK

In this book you will learn why the Mediterranean diet is so healthy, and learn how to incorporate it into your own lifestyle. This book is the follow-up to my first book, *The Mediterranean Diet*, which told of my personal journey, from growing up with the traditional Greek-style Mediterranean diet to researching it as a dietitian at Deakin, Melbourne and La Trobe universities. The book included traditional Greek recipes that my team and I have used in our many clinical studies over the years. These studies have contributed to the large body of evidence that the Mediterranean diet promotes long, healthy lives.

This new book examines the latest evidence of the positive effect on health offered by the Mediterranean diet, with a specific focus on the health benefits of plant foods and a largely plant-based diet, as well as on the advantages of intermittent fasting. The large recipe section offers a broader range of traditional dishes, including those from other Mediterranean countries such as Italy and Spain. You should find them enjoyable to cook and to share with your family and friends.

# Part One

## The
# Mediterranean
# Diet

# 1. Comparing the Mediterranean diets

There is not just one type of Mediterranean diet, but as many as there are countries bordering the Mediterranean Sea. To date, the diet of seven Mediterranean countries – Greece, Cyprus, Italy, Spain, Croatia, Morocco and Portugal – has been recognised by UNESCO as part of the 'Intangible Cultural Heritage of Humanity'. This acknowledges the vital importance of the traditional Mediterranean cuisine to the health and wellbeing of Mediterranean people. In the words of the UNESCO committee, 'The Mediterranean diet emphasizes values of hospitality, neighbourliness, intercultural dialogue and creativity, and a way of life guided by respect for diversity.'

The traditional Greek (or Cretan) diet was first recognised for its protective effects against heart disease in the 1950s, by American scientist Ancel Keys. His Seven Countries Study demonstrated that Cretans lived longer than other populations and had very low rates of heart disease. He attributed these happy outcomes to their diet. Ever since this groundbreaking study, there has been a steady stream of research into the health benefits of both the Cretan and other Mediterranean diets.

# WHAT ALL MEDITERRANEAN DIETS HAVE IN COMMON

Despite the many differences in the cuisines of the Mediterranean countries, they all share these key health-promoting ingredients:

- *extra virgin olive oil as the main dietary fat*
- *fresh vegetables especially leafy greens, tomatoes, onions and garlic*
- *fresh or dried herbs and spices*
- *legumes*
- *nuts*
- *a moderately low meat intake and moderate intake of eggs and dairy*
- *a moderate alcohol intake.*

The three most common Mediterranean cuisines in Australia are Greek, Italian and Spanish.

## The Greek (Cretan) Mediterranean diet

Until fairly recently, most Greek restaurants served entrées of creamy dips and fried cheese with copious amounts of bread, followed by enormous platters of charcoal-grilled meats with a side of fried potatoes and the obligatory Greek salad with its large block of feta cheese. Traditionally, this type of eating was considered a feast, taken on special days such as Christmas and Easter. But this is all vastly different from the largely plant-based traditional Greek diet.

The Cretan Mediterranean diet is considered the 'archetypal' Mediterranean diet. Its cuisine relies on an abundance of plant foods such as fresh fruits and vegetables (particularly leafy greens, tomatoes, onions and garlic), nuts, legumes, unprocessed cereals; moderate portions of red meat and dairy (mainly consumed as feta-style cheese and yoghurt); fish and seafood (in coastal villages); extra virgin olive oil as the main source of fat; and wine enjoyed regularly with meals.

A typical day in the traditional Greek menu consisted of freshly boiled milk (usually goat's), with a dry rusk (called *paximadi*) drizzled with olive oil and sometimes chopped tomato and onion and a little cheese (either feta or *mitzithra* – fresh cheese made from milk and whey from ewe's or goat's milk). This was called *dakos* and a similar version in the Italian cuisine is *bruschetta*. The mid-morning snack included a strong black Greek coffee with another *paximadi* or other small biscuit made with olive oil. Lunch was usually the largest meal and consisted of small portions of meat (usually goat or rabbit) or baked or fried fish with plenty of seasonal vegetables (salads and cooked wild edible greens or *horta*) dressed with olive oil. Vegetarian meals were common with legumes as the main protein source as meat was scarce. A glass of homemade wine was also common. After the meal, seasonal fresh fruit and nuts were served as the dessert with a Greek coffee and this was then followed by an afternoon nap. Evening meals were usually lighter and followed a walk down to the local πλατεια or square where people gathered. Evening meals consisted of soups with legumes (such as lentil soup or *fassoulada*) with crusty bread or a small plate of sardines or anchovies, a few olives, some cheese, a salad and some bread.

## The Italian Mediterranean diet

The modern interpretation of the Italian diet we see in restaurants includes an abundance of carbohydrate-rich foods such as pizza and pasta dishes, often served with buttered bread and very few salads or vegetables. Although bread has long been a staple of traditional Italian cuisine, like the Greeks, the Italians ate wholegrain sourdough bread rather than fluffy white yeast bread or dense, oily focaccia.

The traditional Italian diet was very similar to the Cretan Mediterranean diet. It was rich in cereals, vegetables, fruits and vegetable oils, particularly extra virgin olive oil, with a moderate amount of animal products. The intake of alcoholic beverages, mostly wine, was rather high. The notable differences between the Greek and Italian traditional Mediterranean diets were more cereals and wine in Italy and more fruit and olive oil in Greece. The Greeks consumed more fermented dairy foods, such as yoghurt and feta cheese, rather than the hard cheeses of Italy.

A typical day of the traditional Italian diet consisted of three main meals with a snack in the afternoon. Breakfast was usually an espresso coffee with hot milk (caffe latte or cappuccino) with a sweet pastry or biscuit, or a small bread roll with cheese and a slice of cured meat (*panino*). Lunch was normally the main meal of the day followed by a rest period as for the Greeks. The Italian lunch, however, comprised multiple courses – such as the first plate (*primo piatto*), usually a pasta dish or rice dish (*risotto*); followed by a second dish (*secondo piatto*), a braised meat or fish dish with vegetables or salad; followed by fruit and hard cheese (parmesan or provolone). Italians would usually have a mid-afternoon snack of a sweet pastry or biscuit with an espresso (short black) coffee, fruit or nuts. The evening meal was usually light and including a soup (minestrone) or cold meats and cheese with bread, or leftovers from lunch. Wine (usually homemade red) was often enjoyed with meals. Popular quick Italian meals included the well-known pizza.

## The Spanish Mediterranean diet

The Spanish Mediterranean diet is characterised by extra virgin olive oil as the main fat, ripe tomatoes and capsicums, salad greens, garlic and onions, fresh seafood, plenty of legumes (especially chick peas), rice, bread and homemade red wines.

The Spanish Mediterranean diet was made famous in scientific circles by the Prevencion con Dieta Mediterranean (PREDIMED) study involving 7500 people who were overweight and had some heart disease risk factors. The participants either followed a traditional Mediterranean diet, supplemented with nuts and extra virgin olive oil, over five years or were provided with advice on a low-fat diet. Those who followed the Spanish Mediterranean diet had a 30 per cent lower risk of death from heart disease and a 52 per cent lower risk of developing diabetes.

The traditional daily eating pattern in Spain was typically Mediterranean, comprising a small breakfast of bread, olives, tomato, coffee with milk (often the only milk Spanish adults consumed); a larger lunch of multiple dishes shared in a social gathering, followed by a siesta; and a late light supper, usually after a long walk.

Unfortunately, in recent years dietary patterns in Spain have changed (as they have in Greece and Italy) and people are eating more meat (especially processed meat like jamón, which used to be an occasional treat) and drinking more beer. In some areas of Spain the government is working hard to return people to their traditional eating habits.

## A DEFINITION OF THE MEDITERRANEAN DIET

The illustration below summarises the main characteristics of all Mediterranean diets, with information on the types of foods eaten, serving sizes and frequency. This image incorporates the whole lifestyle of Mediterranean people, including regular physical activity, relaxation and social gatherings – around food, of course!

## The Mediterranean diet summarised

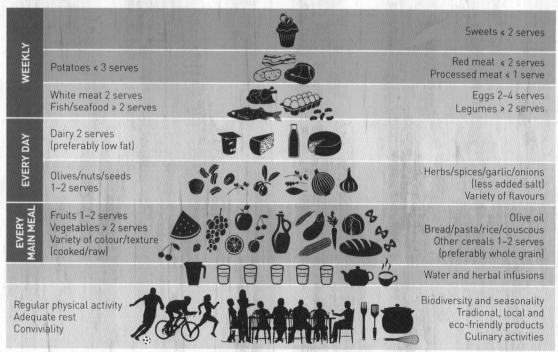

| | |
|---|---|
| | Sweets ≤ 2 serves |
| **WEEKLY** Potatoes ≤ 3 serves | Red meat ≤ 2 serves / Processed meat ≤ 1 serve |
| White meat 2 serves / Fish/seafood ≥ 2 serves | Eggs 2–4 serves / Legumes ≥ 2 serves |
| **EVERY DAY** Dairy 2 serves (preferably low fat) | |
| Olives/nuts/seeds 1–2 serves | Herbs/spices/garlic/onions (less added salt) / Variety of flavours |
| **EVERY MAIN MEAL** Fruits 1–2 serves / Vegetables ≥ 2 serves / Variety of colour/texture (cooked/raw) | Olive oil / Bread/pasta/rice/couscous / Other cereals 1–2 serves (preferably whole grain) |
| | Water and herbal infusions |
| Regular physical activity / Adequate rest / Conviviality | Biodiversity and seasonality / Tradional, local and eco-friendly products / Culinary activities |

*Serving size based on frugality and local habits. Wine in moderation and respecting social beliefs.*

# 2. A healthy diet – the latest evidence

The many health benefits of the Mediterranean diet have been repeatedly proven. These include reduced chronic disease and reduced mortality. A search of the scientific literature quickly reveals more than 3000 scientific articles on the health benefits of the Mediterranean diet, and new evidence emerges every day.

A large meta-analysis (analysis of pooled data from all published studies to determine any overall effect) of data from more than 2 million people worldwide demonstrated that closer adherence to a Mediterranean-style diet is associated with a 10 per cent reduction in the risk of death from cardiovascular disease (heart disease and stroke), 6 per cent reduction in death from cancer, and 13 per cent reduction in the incidence of neurodegenerative diseases such as Alzheimer's and Parkinson's disease.

## CARDIOVASCULAR DISEASE AND DIABETES

The most compelling evidence of the health benefits of the Mediterranean diet comes from the PREDIMED study, which ran from 2003 to 2011. Involving almost 7500 people from 50 different study sites across Spain, it was the largest ever trial involving disease prevention through diet. The people recruited to the study were aged 55–80 and all had risk factors for heart disease. They were assigned randomly to one of three groups. The first group was given advice on a low-fat, high-carbohydrate diet (the control group), while the other two groups were given advice (dietary training) on the Mediterranean diet, along with one of two free foods, either 1 litre of extra virgin olive oil per week or 30 grams per day of nuts (walnuts, hazelnuts, almonds). This study did not specifically focus on reducing calorie (kilojoule) intake to achieve weight loss nor did it focus on physical activity.

At the end of the study the results were remarkable; those who followed either Mediterranean diet had a 30 per cent lower risk of dying of cardiovascular disease and a 52 per cent reduction in the risk of developing diabetes compared with the control group. Importantly, these beneficial effects of the Mediterranean diet occurred even if the participant lost no weight.

A recent report from the study showed that those on the Mediterranean diet supplemented with nuts had a 40 per cent lower chance of developing depression. Furthermore, a report from this study on more than 500 older men and women (average age 74 years) found that those on either of the Mediterranean diets had better cognitive function (memory, thinking and ability to do complex tasks) after five years on the diet compared to those in the control group following a low-fat diet.

# Weight loss: the Mediterranean diet versus low-fat and low-carb diets

All weight-loss diets work by creating an energy deficit – in other words, when we consume less energy than we expend, we lose weight. Most studies on weight loss are short-term – six weeks or three months – and the effects in the longer term are often not monitored. When they are, the disappointing news is that for the overwhelming majority weight loss is not sustained. People creep back to their old habits and usually regain any weight they lost by the end of the first year. Often they end up heavier than when they started.

One well-controlled study of obese middle-aged men and women in Israel ran over two years and compared the effectiveness for weight loss of three diets: a low-fat diet; a-high protein, low-carbohydrate diet; and a Mediterranean diet.

The low-fat diet followed the American Heart Association guidelines: 30 per cent of energy (calories or kilojoules) from fat and less than 10 per cent of this fat from saturated (animal) fats; and a low energy intake – 6300 kilojoules (1500 kcal) for women and 7500 kilojoules (1800 kcal) for men. The diet consisted of low-fat whole grains, vegetables, fruits and legumes; avoidance of sweets and high-fat snacks; and minimal added fats (generally polyunsaturated margarines).

The low-carbohydrate diet did not restrict protein or fat (although a vegetarian style of eating was recommended) but heavily restricted carbohydrate, initially to an extremely low 20 grams per day (one piece of fruit or one slice of bread) rising to a maximum of 120 grams per day (about half what most people normally eat).

The Mediterranean diet used in this study was moderately high in fat (35 per cent of calories/kilojoules) with a focus on vegetables, fish, olive oil and nuts, and less meat and poultry.

After two years of follow-up the researchers found that all participants lost weight. Those in the Mediterranean group and the low-carbohydrate group, however, lost significantly more (double that of the low-fat group). Interestingly, the low-carbohydrate group lost the most weight in the first six months (6.5 kg compared to 5 kg for the Mediterranean diet group) but they regained weight faster than the other groups. The Mediterranean diet group, in contrast, lost weight and kept it off for the two years. This was probably due to the filling nature of the diet and the fact that the participants enjoyed the diet so much they did not deviate from it. In addition, those on the Mediterranean diet who had diabetes enjoyed better diabetes control after two years than those on the other diets.

## FATTY LIVER

Fatty liver is the abnormal accumulation of fat in the liver and occurs in 20–30 per cent of the population. It's more common among people with diabetes and high blood cholesterol, and almost all obese people have some form of fatty liver. Fatty liver leads to many complications such as type 2 diabetes, and may even lead to liver cancer.

In a recent study we conducted in Australia among people with fatty liver, led by gastroenterologist Dr Marno Ryan, we compared the effects of a traditional Mediterranean diet to a low-fat, high-carbohydrate diet and found that after six weeks on the Mediterranean diet, levels of liver fat fell by almost 40 per cent, whereas the low-fat diet yielded only a small 7 per cent change. Insulin resistance (a precursor to diabetes and common symptom of fatty liver) significantly improved on the Mediterranean diet and there was no change on the low-fat diet. These effects were seen even without weight loss – it was purely the effect of the Mediterranean diet.

Until very recently, there had been no well-established dietary treatment for this condition, but we at La Trobe University are continuing our work on using the Mediterranean diet against fatty liver with a large group of doctors, dietitians and other researchers, led by my colleague Dr Audrey Tierney and involving our PhD scholar Elena Papamiltiadous.

## LONGEVITY

A Mediterranean-style diet is not only associated with an extended lifespan but more importantly healthy ageing. The longest living populations around the world occur in five regions, dubbed 'blue zones', including Japan (Okinawans), Italy (Sardinians), California (Seventh Day Adventists), Costa Rica (Nicoyans) and Greece (Ikarians). In two of these regions, Sardinia and Icaria, the people eat a traditional Mediterranean diet, but all five regions share key diet and lifestyle factors associated with longevity:

- *family coherence*
- *no smoking*
- *an active social life*
- *very low levels of stress*
- *regular physical activity, and*
- *a plant-based diet.*

One of the first studies to demonstrate that closer adherence to a Mediterranean-style diet is linked to longevity was by Professor Antonia Trichopoulou from the University of Athens. Using the Mediterranean diet score co-developed by Australian Associate Professor Antigone Kouris-Blazos, they showed that a two-point increase in the score (which ranges from 0 for no adherence to the diet to 9 for maximal adherence) was linked to a 36 per cent reduction in death from any cause.

## Longevity and alcohol consumption

An important part of the Mediterranean diet is regular consumption of moderate amounts of wine (up to two glasses a day for men and one glass for women), always with food. This 'Mediterranean way of drinking' has been linked to lower death rates from all causes in many populations, including recently in northern Europeans. It has also been suggested as the main explanation of the 'French paradox'. In France people have low rates of death from heart disease despite a relatively high-fat diet (particularly in the north of France), with lots of animal foods such as creamy cheeses, butter and rich meats such as duck and pork (with crackling, of course). In their favour, the French eat small portions and rarely snack between meals.

Wine, especially red wine, contains various antioxidants called polyphenols, some of whose names may or may not be familiar to you. They include flavonols such as myricetin and quercetin, catechin and epicatechin, proanthocyanidins, anthocyanins, various phenolic acids and the stilbene called resveratrol. The positive effect of resveratrol is no doubt due to its antioxidant, anti-inflammatory and anti-carcinogenic properties. It rescues cells from damage and helps them live longer by increasing levels of an important enzyme called sirtuin 1 that helps stop damage to DNA from stress.

## Longevity and DNA

Ageing is caused by the gradual deterioration in the ability of our cells to reproduce faithfully. The number of times each cell reproduces is regulated by DNA buffers on the chromosomes called telomeres. Each time a cell reproduces, the telomeres get shorter, until eventually the cell can no longer divide. Reduction in telomere length can be accelerated by oxidative stress and inflammation that are known to cause cell damage.

Researchers from Harvard University in the United States recently analysed the links between diet and telomere length in almost 5000 women enrolled in the Nurses Health Study, which has been examining the diet and lifestyle of 121,000 American nurses since the 1970s. The researchers found that the women who followed a Mediterranean-style diet had longer telomeres. It would seem that following an anti-inflammatory diet rich in antioxidants, such as the Mediterranean diet, is an ideal way to slow down the ageing process.

## What are *antioxidants* and *free radicals*?

Antioxidants are our natural defence against age-related disease, protecting our cells from harmful free radicals by neutralising them. Free radicals are highly reactive chemicals that if left unchecked can result in oxidative stress and, in turn, cell damage that can lead to conditions such as cancer, diabetes and heart disease. They come from our day-to-day metabolism, cigarette smoke and alcohol.

# 3. The benefits of a plant-based diet

A major concern among health authorities around the world is the rapid movement away from traditional diets towards a more industrialised, refined and highly processed, energy-dense (but nutrient-poor) diet. This 'Western diet' is thought to have led to the worldwide epidemic of obesity and diabetes or 'diabesity'. The governments of Spain, Italy and Greece are establishing specific health campaigns to return people to their traditional diet.

An international study of long-living populations, including those in Greece, Australia (Greek migrants and Anglo-Celtic Australians), Finland and Japan, found that Australian Greek migrants lived the longest. Unlike their contemporaries they left behind in Greece, these people have maintained their important traditional diet. Perhaps surprisingly, the consumption of legumes (beans and pulses) was the most important predictor of longevity across all these population groups.

## The Mediterranean diet through the ages

The key elements of the Mediterranean diet span thousands of years. We know from Ancient Greek literature and art that the Ancient Mediterranean diet was based on the 'Mediterranean triad' of wheat, olive oil and wine. Unleavened bread made from wheat and, more importantly, barley (which was more abundant and easier to grow) was a staple. Vegetables were abundant and included cabbage, onions, garlic, wild edible greens (*horta*), peas, beans, broad beans, and many dried pulses, such as lentils and chick peas, which were often the main protein source in meals. Fresh or dried fruits (figs, raisins, pomegranates), legumes and nuts (chestnuts, dried chick peas, dried broad beans and lupins) were eaten for dessert or as snacks. In coastal regions people ate fish (sardines, tuna, red mullet, swordfish and eels) and seafood (octopus, squid and shellfish). Chickens and quails were bred for their eggs, and delicacies such as pheasant eggs were also eaten. Meats were often game meats (hare and birds), while wealthier people bred goats, pigs and sheep. Dairy products were mainly yoghurt, ricotta or mizithra, and feta made from goat or sheep's milk. Herbs and spices were used extensively in cooking and were revered for their medicinal properties.

Although the tomato and tomato products are considered key ingredients of the traditional Mediterranean diet, the fruit was only introduced into Europe in the 1500s after the colonisation of the Americas, where it originated. (The same is true of eggplants, capsicums, potatoes and chillies.) The southern Europeans rapidly incorporated the tasty tomato into their cuisines – the Italians called it *pomo d'oro*, or 'golden apple'. In northern Europe and Britain, by contrast, people rejected it for many years. Some even believed it was poisonous.

# THE POWER OF PLANTS

Scientists recently analysed all studies conducted between 1950 to 2013 on the ability of certain food groups and beverages to protect against diet-related chronic conditions such as obesity, type 2 diabetes, cardiovascular disease, depression, Alzheimer's disease, Parkinson's disease, general cognitive decline, cancers, osteoporosis and kidney disease. The analysis showed that plant foods are more effective than animal foods in preventing obesity, type 2 diabetes, cardiovascular disease and cancer.

Within the plant food groups, grains (including wholegrain cereals, nuts, seeds and legumes) were more protective than fruits and vegetables. Tea was found to be protective overall, whereas coffee only protected against type 2 diabetes. Within the animal food groups, dairy foods were neutral while red or processed meats increased the risk of chronic diseases.

These findings strongly support the value of a Mediterranean diet, which encourages consumption of vegetables, legumes, fruits and nuts, cereals and fish, while moderating consumption of meat, poultry and dairy products.

## The ratio of plant to animal food

In the traditional Mediterranean diet the ratio from plant foods to animal foods is 4:1 by volume or weight. In the modern Australian diet, by contrast, it is about 2:1.

Until recently, the focus of research into the Mediterranean diet has been the low intake of animal fat and high intake of olive oil. Although the type of fat and the food source of that fat eaten is important, it's now thought that the most important aspect of the Mediterranean diet is the high ratio of plant to animal food as well as the type and variety of plant foods eaten. The Cretan men in Ancel Keys' landmark Seven Countries Study consumed four times more plant foods than animal foods. Their diets were rich in phytochemicals (i.e. plant chemicals) with antioxidant, anti-inflammatory, and anti-carcinogenic effects. These included polyphenols from extra virgin olive oil, wine, nuts and legumes; and numerous phytochemicals from leafy greens (including wild plants), tomatoes, onions, herbs and spices. These phytochemicals could play a significant role in reducing chronic disease, particularly cardiovascular disease.

Because plant foods are bulky – that is, they are filling but lower in energy density – they assist in weight loss and diabetes prevention. The diets of Ancel Keys' Cretan men included about 500 grams of fruit (3–4 serves) and 500 grams of vegetables (5–6 serves) per day, as well as a sizeable quantity of wholegrain sourdough bread. After all this roughage, there was no room for snacking on sweets or high-fat savoury snacks.

One of my own studies involved giving the traditional Mediterranean diet to middle-aged Australian-born men and women with type 2 diabetes. We found that participants really enjoyed the diet and never felt hungry – some even found it hard to eat all the food. After three months on the diet, their diabetes control improved, some lost weight, the levels of plant-derived antioxidants in their blood increased, they felt more energetic, and they did not want to return to their usual diet.

In our own studies of elderly Greek migrants to Australia with diabetes, led by my colleague Associate Professor Laima Brazionis, we found that Greek migrants appeared to be protected from some of the complications of diabetes, such as diabetic retinopathy, compared to Australian-born people with diabetes and we hypothesised that this is partly due to their close adherence to a traditional plant-based Mediterranean diet rich in plant-derived phytochemicals, including a wide range of antioxidants.

## Polyphenols

Polyphenols are bioactive chemicals mainly found in plant foods and plant-derived beverages such as coffee, tea and red wine. A recent analysis of data from the PREDIMED study investigated the link between dietary intake of polyphenols and death over the five years of the study. The analysis showed that people who consumed large quantities of polyphenols, especially those from extra virgin olive oil (the lignans oleuropein and hydroxytyrosol) and red wine (the stilbene resveratrol), had a 37 per cent lower risk of dying from any cause than those who consumed less of these polyphenols. The effect of these polyphenols was cumulative – all plant foods and beverages high in polyphenols were important, including herbs, spices, legumes, green tea, nuts, seeds and extra virgin olive oil.

Some polyphenols and their derivatives can protect against hardening of the arteries and reduce inflammation in the cells that line the blood vessels.

## HERBS, SPICES AND ANTIOXIDANTS

Herbs and spices are terms often used interchangeably but the term 'herb' is generally used to mean fresh or dried leaves while 'spice' is used to denote dried and often ground non-leafy plant components (such as seeds and fruits).

Herbs and spices have been used for culinary and medicinal purposes for thousands of years, including in Ancient Greece and Rome. Hippocrates (460–377 BC), known as the father of Western medicine and credited with coining the phrase 'Let food be thy medicine and medicine be thy food', is known to have used more than 300 herbs and spices in his medicinal treatments. Herbs and spices have also formed the basis of traditional Chinese medicine and Indian Ayurvedic traditional medicine, both of which date back thousands of years.

Herbs and spices contain concentrated levels of phytochemicals that have antioxidant, anti-inflammatory and anti-carcinogenic properties. Just 1 gram of dried cloves, cinnamon or turmeric, or 5 grams of dried oregano, sage, rosemary, thyme, marjoram or ginger, contains the same level of antioxidants as a 100-gram fruit or vegetable. Herbs and spices have a synergistic effect when combined in a dish, so adding a fresh herb to a salad doubles the antioxidant potential of the meal.

**Many herbs and spices are protective, but some well-known examples include:**

> **GARLIC** *which reduces blood pressure and has anti-blood-clotting effects, therefore protecting against heart attack and stroke*
>
> **LEMONGRASS** *which may reduce blood pressure and also has anti-carcinogenic properties*
>
> **CURCUMIN (the active ingredient in turmeric)** *which has anti-inflammatory effects, improves blood glucose control and has anti-carcinogenic properties, and*
>
> **BASIL, ROSEMARY AND MINT** *all of which have anti-carcinogenic properties.*

Variety is literally the spice of life. Dr Artemis Simopoulos, an endocrinologist and paediatrician, and founder of the Center for Genetics, Nutrition and Health in Washington DC, suggests that a traditional Greek meal is rich in antioxidants because it consists of thirty different ingredients, half of which are culinary herbs and spices.

Just as herbs and spices are good for human health, they are also good for animals. Free-range animals are healthier, and their meat is lean and healthy because they are allowed to roam free, exercise and eat a varied diet rich in healthy fats (from plants) and herbs. This type of free-range diet, rich in plant-derived antioxidants, improves not only the health of these animals but also the nutritional quality of their meat.

Professor Kerin O'Dea of the University of South Australia has spent her career investigating the health benefits of indigenous diet cultures. She suggests that the meat from wild animals eaten by the Greeks – specifically the mountain goat – is healthier because it has been 'marinating on the bone' as a result of its diet rich in wild plants and herbs. These animals were truly 'free-range' and had to forage for their food in the wild. Although free-range domesticated animals and their products (eggs and dairy) are healthier than caged or penned animals, the diets of commercially produced modern-day free-range animals can be highly processed and are generally low in antioxidants and healthy fats such as omega-3.

# 4. Food fads versus the Mediterranean diet

**A**lthough the twenty-first century has seen a general desire among those who care about what they eat to move away from processed foods and towards whole foods, in some cases this has led to a faddish reliance on certain types of foods. Examples include the Paleo diet, superfoods and the anti-sugar movement, all of which are discussed in this chapter.

## THE PALEO DIET

The Paleo diet seeks to emulate the diet and lifestyle practices of the people who lived during the Palaeolithic era from 2.5 million to 10,000 years ago. At this time all humans were hunter-gatherers and ate foods they caught, such as meat from wild animals and birds (including organ meat), insects and seafood; and foods they gathered, such as leafy vegetables, roots and nuts. This type of diet was high in protein and relatively low in fat (as wild animals are leaner than domesticated animals), rich in omega-3 fats, low in salt and high in fibre.

It's clear how this diet and lifestyle would promote good health: people were extremely active (hunting and gathering takes an enormous amount of energy) and ate a variety of fresh unprocessed foods without salt, sugars and other additives. Having said that, the life expectancy of humans was about half of what it is today. Many factors have contributed to our longer lifespans today, not the least of them modern medicine, but good nutrition has played a major role.

Paleo diet enthusiasts argue that we are not genetically equipped to digest foods that appeared in our food supply following the agricultural revolution about 10,000 years ago, in particular grains, legumes and dairy foods. They believe we should be eating a diet high in meat, vegetables, fruit and nuts.

## Is the Paleo diet justified?

The concept of Palaeolithic diets first came under scientific discussion during the 1980s, starting with a paper by the American anthropologists S. Boyd Eaton and Melvin Konner. They argued that because humans have not changed significantly in genetic terms during the last 40,000 years, we are therefore genetically programmed to get the most from the diet and lifestyle of our ancestors from 40,000 years ago (the Palaeolithic era). They contended that as a species we have not yet had time to adapt to the major changes to our diet and lifestyle as a result of agriculture, the Industrial Revolution, and modern food processing.

But the fact is that humans have continued to evolve and adapt to their environment. Although our genes have not changed substantially in 40,000 years, there have been some important genetic changes in the last 10,000 years since the advent of agriculture, such as those enabling humans to digest milk or carbohydrates from grains. In her book *Paleofantasy*, evolutionary biologist Dr Marlene Zuk from the University of Minnesota dispels the Paleo diet theories. She describes human evolution as opportunistic and explains how humans do evolve to new environments in order to survive. When people began to herd cattle and harvest their milk, for example, they evolved the gene that codes for the milk-digesting enzyme lactase, which allowed them to develop tolerance over time to this nutrient-rich fluid.

The modern-day Paleo diet focuses heavily on meat and what enthusiasts consider to be more natural fats, such as coconut oil and butter.

Unless very lean meats are eaten and processed meats avoided, excess meat in the diet often leads to a higher intake of animal fat. Also consider that Palaeolithic man was unlikely to have eaten coconut oil, which grows only in the tropics and requires extraction, or butter, which only appeared after humans began farming cattle during the Neolithic era.

There is no good evidence to support the avoidance of grains and legumes in the diet on the grounds of health, weight management or longevity. Humans have been consuming grains and legumes for more than 20,000 years. As we have seen, a recent extensive review of all studies on diet and diet-related chronic disease between 1950 and 2013 reported that plant foods were more protective against diet-related chronic diseases, such as cardiovascular disease, diabetes, cancer and digestive diseases, than animal foods; and that among plant foods, grains (including wholegrain cereals, nuts and legumes) were the most protective. While dairy products were neutral, red and processed meats tended to increase the risk of these chronic diseases.

## Is there any scientific evidence for the Paleo diet?

Very few studies (less than ten) have examined the weight loss and health benefits of a Paleo diet compared with other diets, and the general quality of these studies is not high. Although the studies have shown positive effects of the Paleo diet on blood cholesterol and blood pressure, these changes were most likely due to weight loss rather than the specific components of the diet itself. The Paleo diet is also more expensive and difficult to reproduce due to changes in the food supply.

The CSIRO Total Wellbeing Diet is similar to the Paleo diet in that it's a high-protein, moderate-carbohydrate diet focused on lean meat and fish and plenty of low-starch leafy vegetables. Extensive research has demonstrated its benefits in weight loss and general health, although some people find it hard to follow due to the large quantities of meat, which also make it more expensive than a largely plant-based diet.

## SUPERFOODS

The term 'superfoods' is essentially a buzzword applied in the media to individual foods or ingredients and implying that these foods offer specific and powerful health benefits. It's not a term used in the scientific literature. *The Oxford Dictionary* defines a superfood as 'A nutrient-rich food considered to be especially beneficial for health and well-being.'

While the term is often applied to fad foods such as goji berries or wheatgrass, a superfood can basically be any food that is rich in nutrients, such as oily fish like salmon, antioxidant-rich fruits such as blueberries or pomegranates, and wild edible leafy greens dressed with extra virgin olive oil. Frankly, the Mediterranean diet includes an abundance of such foods.

No single food, however, can be a cure-all or a magic bullet. When people focus on including a particular superfood in their diet – such as snacking on goji berries or adding kale to their salads – they can be in danger of paying insufficient attention to the rest of their diet. A poor diet plus one superfood is still a poor diet. Even fish oil supplements, which have been shown to be effective against many chronic diseases such as heart disease and osteoarthritis, are not that effective in combination with a poor diet. Nutrient-rich foods and ingredients work synergistically to provide their full health benefit.

We would do better to focus on 'super diets' rich in plant-based bioactive nutrients, healthy oils from fish and nuts, and fermented dairy foods with antioxidant, anti-inflammatory and anti-carcinogenic properties. Having said that, the Mediterranean diet includes several foods that could be described as superfoods because they are particularly rich in nutrients. These include extra virgin olive oil, garlic, walnuts and broccoli.

### Extra virgin olive oil

This key ingredient in the Mediterranean diet helps prevent heart disease through its high monounsaturated-fat content, which maintains the level of HDL or 'good' cholesterol in the blood. It's also renowned for its role in promoting longevity, a quality attributable to its high levels of polyphenols (see page 18). Extra virgin olive oil also has a high concentration of a naturally occurring anti-inflammatory substance called oleocanthal, which gives the oil its peppery taste and that sting in the back of the throat. Oleocanthal has similar properties to the anti-inflammatory drug ibuprofen.

When buying extra virgin olive oil, make sure you select one of the highest quality. It's best fresh (less than one year since harvest) and its quality can be maintained by storing it in a cool dark place away from light, heat and air exposure (oxygen), which can cause oxidation and thus deterioration. Pure olive oils, light or extra light are refined olive oils with small quantities of extra virgin olive oil added for flavour. Although these oils have the same calorie content as extra virgin olive oil, they have a much milder taste and are very poor sources of polyphenols and other antioxidant substances.

## Garlic

This favourite aromatic vegetable or herb has been used by many cultures around the world as herbal medicine for thousands of years. Garlic contains a chemical called allicin that has antibacterial, antifungal and antiviral properties. Garlic may also be beneficial in preventing heart disease by helping reduce blood pressure and LDL or 'bad' cholesterol.

## Walnuts

These tasty nuts are packed with many nutrients that are protective for heart disease and other chronic diseases. Walnuts are one of the few nuts that contain alpha-linolenic acid (ALA), the plant form of the omega-3 oils that are so important for heart health. Walnuts also contain L-arginine, a protein that can boost immune function; and resveratrol, an antioxidant that protects against cell damage and inflammation. Walnuts, and also almonds and hazelnuts, are also rich in polyphenols (if you eat the skin).

## Broccoli

This green favourite belongs to a family of vegetables called crucifers (which includes cabbage, Brussels sprouts and cauliflower), all of which have been shown in many population studies to be associated with protection from cancer, especially prostate cancer. The key protective chemical in broccoli and related vegetables, called sulforaphane, is thought to protect against cancer by selectively targeting cancer cells, then engulfing and destroying them while leaving healthy cells alone.

## AVOIDING SUGAR

Several popular authors advocate cutting sugar out of the diet completely, calling it a poison as addictive as heroin. The truth is, sugar is not a toxic substance. What we generally call sugar (white sugar, raw sugar or brown sugar) is known scientifically as sucrose, a simple carbohydrate that is broken down in the body by digestion to the simplest sugars glucose and fructose. All simple sugars taste sweet and are a basic source of energy in the diet.

That's not to say that sugar is particularly good for you. While sugar provides the same amount of energy as other carbohydrate foods such as bread, pasta, rice, starchy vegetables and fruit, on its own it has no bulk, vitamins, minerals or fibre to make it filling or nutritious. Sugar is often used in processed foods as a sweetener, to add colour (caramelised sugar), as a bulking agent or as a preservative (because bacteria do not thrive in concentrated sugar solutions).

Small amounts of sugar in the diet are not harmful. The general recommendation is that sugar should not provide any more than 10 per cent of our daily energy requirements. For women that would be about 50 grams (about 3 tablespoons) of sugar and for men about 65 grams (about 4 tablespoons) of sugar a day. The World Health Organization has just released a report recommending added sugars be reduced to less than 10 per cent of total energy and preferably as low as 5 per cent, half what was previously recommended. On average, however, Australians are eating more than three times this quantity – more than 50 kilograms of sugar per person per year. Much of this sugar comes 'hidden' in the form of soft drinks.

The problem with excess sugar is that it adversely affects the quality of the diet, raising its energy content but reducing its nutrient content. In other words, it provides empty calories.

Added sugar appears on food labels in many forms, such as sucrose, glucose, fructose, maltose, dextrose, glucose syrup and high-fructose corn syrup, so it's important to read labels carefully if you need to cut down on your sugar intake. It's also important to consider that dried fruit is high in naturally occurring sugars, and milk and yoghurt contain a natural sugar called lactose. There is no reason to be alarmed by naturally occurring sugars in fresh fruits, yoghurt or milk, although people that need to carefully monitor their carbohydrate intake, such as those with type 1 or type 2 diabetes, will need to consult their GP and Accredited Practising Dietitian for individualised advice.

## The real trouble with sugar

The amount of added sugar in the Western diet has continued to increase dramatically in the last 100 years, and this has been linked with worldwide epidemics of obesity, metabolic syndrome and diabetes.

A recent review of 32 studies from around the world involving more than 200,000 children and adults found that consumption of one serving (355 ml) of sugar-sweetened beverages per day was associated with a weight gain of almost 1 kilogram per year in adults and the equivalent in children.

Another review of multiple studies involving more than 300,000 participants demonstrated that people consuming 1–2 servings (355–710 ml) of sweetened beverages per day had a 26 per cent greater risk of developing type 2 diabetes than those consuming none or less than one serving per month.

As if all that were not bad enough, added sugars, particularly in sweetened beverages, are well known to cause dental caries.

## Sugar and the Mediterranean diet

In his original Seven Countries Study, Ancel Keys found that those in the Mediterranean region who regularly consumed sugar in the form of sweets, cakes and pastries had an increased risk of dying of heart disease. The Cretan people, however, had a very low intake of added refined sugar because they only ate sweets, cakes and pastries on special occasions. The majority of sugars in their diet came from fresh fruits and honey.

The modernised Mediterranean diet pyramid (see page 7) recommends less than two serves of sweets a week. This means that following a Mediterranean diet ensures that your intake of added sugars is very low.

Greeks traditionally use honey to sweeten cakes, biscuits and hot beverages such as tea. Adding sugar to sweets is considered a cheap alternative. Honey is also a high-energy food, and can contribute to weight gain and disease, but it contains trace amounts of antioxidants, vitamins and minerals.

# 5. Healthy fasting on the Mediterranean diet

Fasting can mean anything from not eating or drinking for a specific period of time to excluding certain foods on an ongoing basis or for a specific period. From a cultural historical perspective, fasting has often been related to a religious event. This can involve periods of complete abstinence from food and drink for specific periods of time, such as Ramadan, where no food or drink is consumed during daylight hours throughout the forty-day fasting period; or a restrictive fast such as the Greek Orthodox custom of eating a completely vegan diet during numerous fasting periods (such as the forty-eight days before Easter), or on a regular weekly basis such as Wednesdays and Fridays. In religious terms, fasting is seen as a means of growing closer to God, of purification, of commemorative mourning or of gratitude. In some faiths it's also used to help achieve atonement.

We as researchers find fasting practices of particular interest with regard to weight loss and metabolic health. Many involve avoiding meat, other animal products and alcohol, and therefore dramatically reduce the intake of animal fat, cholesterol, alcohol and calories in general. Ramadan fasting involves periods of eight to ten hours without food. This can have dramatic effects on metabolism as the body soon adapts to using internal sources of energy from glycogen (carbohydrate stores) and fat stores.

# THE SCIENCE OF FASTING

Research into fasting has focused primarily on the effects of prolonged energy restriction on weight loss, health and longevity. Prolonged energy restriction is generally defined as consuming 20–40 per cent less energy than you would normally consume if you weren't thinking about it. Mild energy restriction (but not malnutrition) is the only non-genetic strategy that has been consistently shown to extend life in animal studies. In human studies, prolonged energy restriction has been shown to be beneficial in overweight people for improving heart disease risk factors and insulin sensitivity (and therefore the risk of type 2 diabetes), while also reducing oxidative damage to DNA and so having the potential to extend life. Short-term severe energy restriction (600 kcal per day) has been shown to reverse type 2 diabetes in the early phases as shown by a study of middle-aged men and women with type 2 diabetes.

Despite these benefits, prolonged energy restriction is unsustainable, as we are constantly fighting our hunger and a general desire to eat more. A feedback loop also kicks in to protect us from weight loss by signalling the body to eat more and exercise less in order to conserve energy and maintain weight. This is often referred to as our body weight 'set point'.

## INTERMITTENT FASTING

The unsustainability of prolonged energy restriction has led to a focus on intermittent fasting, which involves restricting food intake (to as low as 10–25 per cent of energy needs) on one or two days each week and eating normally (or even feasting) on the other days. Studies of intermittent fasting in animals date back to the 1940s and show similar beneficial effects on weight and metabolic health to prolonged energy restriction. Human studies have been promising, although the results show that it's more effective in obese and overweight people and in people with diabetes or fatty liver. We don't yet know what the long-term beneficial effects of continuous energy restriction or intermittent fasting might be on healthy people of normal weight.

Insufficient regular nutrition due to intermittent fasting places stress on the cells. This is thought to trigger an adaptive response that enhances their ability to cope with this stress and thus to counteract disease. The exact mechanism of this response is not yet known but is the subject of much new research.

According to some studies, following the initial uncomfortable phase of hunger and cravings, the brain seems to adapt and overcome our addiction to regular food consumption through the day. This means that we become used to the feeling of hunger and are less driven to eat based on hunger cues. This only continues to be effective for the body and for weight loss if the fast remains intermittent rather than constant. In other words, although not eating on one or two days works, increasing your fasting days beyond this will actually be detrimental and dangerous.

## The 5:2 diet fast for weight loss

The popular 5:2 diet is a typical example of an intermittent fast or alternate-day fasting regime. This diet involves one to three non-consecutive 'fast days' each week upon which energy intake is very low (25 per cent of energy requirements). This translates to an average total of 500 calories (2100 kJ) per day for women and 600 calories (2500 kJ) per day for men on fast days, alternating with 'feed days' where food is eaten normally.

The 5:2 diet has rapidly gained popularity in recent years because it's relatively easy to follow. Research has shown that a 5:2 type of diet can be as effective in weight loss and metabolic health as continuous energy restriction, and (not surprisingly) the amount of weight lost is dependent on the number of fast days per week. A recent review of intermittent fasting diet trials has shown that one fasting day per week can give a 0.25 kilogram weight loss per week while up to three fasting days per week can yield a weight loss of up to 0.75 kilograms per week.

The long-term effectiveness of this diet regime is unknown, as most trials have looked at its effects only over the initial four to six months. It's well known that although people on weight-loss diets can effectively lose 10 per cent of their body weight within a year (10 kilograms or more in overweight or obese people), they tend to return to their original weight or exceed it after two years.

The important thing to remember is that any change you make to your diet and lifestyle must be practical, enjoyable and sustainable. Most diets fail because they are too restrictive and punitive, and eventually everyone gives up. For many people, fasting is simply impractical and antisocial.

## What to expect during an intermittent fast

One six-month study involving 107 overweight women compared weight loss after an intermittent fast of five normal days and two fasting days (5 + 2) each week to weight loss with continuous calorie restriction (i.e. a 'traditional' weight-loss diet). The study found that the 5 + 2 diet was just as effective for weight loss (the average weight loss was about 6 kilograms in each). Both diets also led to similar improvements in risk factors for diabetes and cardiovascular disease, such as reduced blood fats, blood pressure and blood glucose, and improved insulin control.

The women on the 5 + 2 diet, however, experienced more side effects. They complained of feeling hungry, lacking energy, feeling cold, headaches and constipation. They also reported lack of concentration, bad temper, preoccupation with food, and trouble fitting the diet into their normal routine.

Given these potential side effects, anyone attempting the 5 + 2 diet would be advised to carefully plan their fasting days to coincide with low-activity days. It's probably not a good idea, for example, to fast on a day when you need to stay focused for, say, an exam, an important presentation at work or a long drive. The same is true of a job where you regularly operate any type of machinery that requires your complete attention.

If you do undertake an intermittent fast, make sure you stay well hydrated during the fasting days. There's no need to avoid drinking water; in fact, water may help alleviate some of the symptoms of hunger, cravings and lack of concentration.

## Who shouldn't attempt intermittent fasting

Intermittent fasting or alternate-day fasting is not recommended for children, pregnant or breastfeeding women, the very old, and underweight or very unwell people.

People taking any form of medication or undergoing medical treatment should consult their doctor before attempting an intermittent fasting diet or any other very restrictive diet. Many medications require regular consumption of food, and prolonged periods of fasting can make them dangerous. People with type 2 diabetes, for example, who are on anti-diabetic (oral hypoglycaemic) medication or insulin injections may be at risk of hypoglycaemia (dangerously low blood sugar levels) on fasting days. Other medications such as steroids or antidepressants can also cause side effects during fasting days. It's always best to check with your doctor before attempting any fasting diet.

Many religious faiths will exempt anyone who is sick or taking medications from the need to participate in traditional fasting.

## GREEK ORTHODOX FASTING

Greek Orthodox Christians, like the men from Crete in the Seven Countries Study, may fast for a total of 180–200 days each year, including Lent (the forty-eight days before Easter), the Nativity Fast (the forty days before Christmas), the Assumption (the fifteen days before 15 August) and routinely on Wednesdays and Fridays. This is not complete fasting but more like a restrictive diet and resembles strict vegetarianism or veganism. On certain days, olive oil is avoided and all foods are made without any fat. This type of fasting is more likely to lead to weight loss. Greek Orthodox Christians tend to limit excessive exercise or labour-intensive work during fasting days to retain their strength.

A recent review of Greek Orthodox fasting and health has demonstrated that it can have positive effects on weight and cholesterol, but that prolonged fasting in the elderly may increase the risk of iron-deficiency anaemia. The positive health benefits of Greek Orthodox fasting have been attributed to the reduced intake of saturated fats (from the avoidance of all animal products), and increase in fibre and folate (from the increased intake of fruit, vegetables and legumes).

One of my and Associate Professor Antigone Kouris-Blazos' PhD scholars, Antonia Thodis, is investigating the health and longevity of elderly Greek Islander migrants in Australia. She has found that elderly Greeks are returning to traditional eating and cultural practices as they age, and are fasting more (some more than 150 days per year) and attending church more often. The positive physical health benefits of fasting combined with the positive mental health benefits of the social interaction at church may help explain the longevity and good health experienced by these elderly migrants.

If you would like to attempt an intermittent fast yourself, there are some examples of daily menu plans on page 38.

## A typical *fasting day for* Greek Orthodox Christians

**BREAKFAST:** *Wholegrain sourdough bread with three or four olives and a fresh tomato cut in quarters and sprinkled with herbs, salt and pepper and extra virgin olive oil*

*Herbal tea*

**SNACK:** *Paximadia (dried sweet biscuit made with olive oil) with black coffee or tea*

**LUNCH:** *Fassoulada (bean soup) with sourdough bread and pickled peppers or gherkins and a few olives*

*Glass of water*

**SNACK:** *Fresh or dried fruit and nuts (walnuts, almonds, hazelnuts)*

**DINNER:** *Briami – slow-baked Mediterranean vegetables in a saltsa of olive oil, tomato purée, onion, garlic and fresh herbs and a slice of sourdough bread*

*OR*

*Baked lima bean casserole in a tomato-based sauce, with a few olives and a slice of sourdough bread*

*Glass of water*

*Herbal tea and a small piece of halva*

# 6. Putting the Mediterranean diet into practice

If you have already looked at the pyramid on page 7 and compared the components of the Mediterranean diet to your own diet, you may have discovered that your diet is well on the way to being Mediterranean. You may only need a few tips and the recipes in this book to complete your journey. If your diet didn't include components of the Mediterranean diet, however, read this chapter carefully for tips on how to change your eating patterns.

## USE FRESH INGREDIENTS WITH MINIMAL PROCESSING

Traditional diets and cuisines such as the Mediterranean diet are based on fresh ingredients that are usually cooked within hours of harvesting and marinated or dressed with a variety of culinary herbs and spices. Ingredients are often sourced from home gardens or local markets, and plant varieties are often wild (or in Australia weed) types that are rich in antioxidants.

In a study my research team completed at Deakin University, we compared the levels of certain antioxidants (namely carotenoids such as lycopene, lutein and beta-carotene) in different edible plant species. These included edible green weeds such as sow thistle, amaranth, purslane and dandelion, which we collected from roadsides and home gardens, and commercially available chicory and endive. We found that the levels of lutein and beta-carotene in the wild sow thistle and amaranth were up to 70 per cent higher than in the commercial plants. We also analysed different grades of olive oil (extra virgin, pure and light) and found that extra virgin olive oil had high levels of lutein and beta-carotene while pure olive oil had substantially less and light olive oil had none we could detect.

There is good evidence that we can enhance our absorption of antioxidants from plants by chopping and cooking them, and adding olive oil to the dish. One study, for example, demonstrated that the lycopene content of a tomato dish was increased significantly after the tomato was chopped and puréed, because this released the lycopene from the plant cells. The study also showed that the uptake of lycopene into the body was significantly higher when tomatoes were cooked in extra virgin olive oil than when they were cooked without it. The same has been shown for the uptake of lutein from leafy green vegetables.

## HOW TO READ THE RECIPE NUTRITION TABLES

Each of the recipes in this book includes a nutrition panel to help you plan your meals. These follow the basic pattern of the nutrition panels that are mandatory on food products sold in Australia.

The nutrition panel includes the energy (calorie/kilojoule) content of a single serve and some basic nutritional information, such as the amount of protein, fat (and saturated fat), carbohydrate, fibre and salt (as sodium) the food contains. The panels also include an indication of the proportion of daily requirements of energy and nutrients (protein, fat, carbohydrate and fibre) each serve of a dish contributes on average for men and women. This information will assist with meal planning if you need to follow specific dietary recommendations from your doctor or dietitian.

The daily requirements in the tables are based on what we take to be averages. The figures for women are based on an energy requirement of 8000–8500 kilojoules (1910–2030 kcal) per day, which is the amount expended by a 40-year-old woman with a weight of 65 kilograms and a fairly sedentary office-type job. The figures for men are based on an energy requirement of 10,000–10,500 kilojoules (2390–2510 kcal) per day for a 40-year-old man who weighs about 80 kilograms and has a sedentary office-type job. If these averages do not describe your own age, weight or level of physical activity, you can use the information on energy requirements provided on page 36 to tailor the figures more specifically to your own needs.

Note that what are traditionally referred to as calories are scientifically speaking kilocalories (kcal), or Calories with a capital 'C'. This is why the 'calorie' amounts are given as kcal throughout this book.

# GET THE BALANCE RIGHT MEDITERRANEAN-STYLE

You may already have come across a balanced plate diagram indicating the proportion of vegetables, starchy foods and protein foods you should aim for in a typical meal. The Mediterranean-style balanced plate below indicates a typical meal with a ratio of 4 to 1 of vegetables/salads to meat portions.

*One fifth of the plate* is occupied by lean protein (here Roast Pork Fillet, page 145)

*Half the plate* is taken up by a salad with colourful vegetables, dressed with extra virgin olive oil and fresh lemon juice and herbs (here Northern Greek Salad, page 98)

*The remainder of the plate* is filled with starchy foods (here Slow-baked Root Vegetables in Honey and Balsamic Glaze, page 75)

## Energy requirements for men and women at different ages and activity levels

| GENDER | AGE GROUP | ACTIVITY LEVEL | | |
|--------|-----------|----------------|---|---|
| | | Sedentary | Moderate | High Intensity |
| **FEMALE** | 20–39 | 8492 kJ (2028 kcal) | 10,919 kJ (2608 kcal) | 12,132 kJ (2898 kcal) |
| | 40–69 | 8047 kJ (1922 kcal) | 10,346 kJ (2471 kcal) | 11,496 kJ (2746 kcal) |
| | 70+ | 7315 kJ (1747 kcal) | 9405 kJ (2246 kcal) | 10,450 kJ (2496 kcal) |
| **MALE** | 20–39 | 11,110 kJ (2654 kcal) | 14,285 kJ (3412 kcal) | 15,872 kJ (3791 kcal) |
| | 40–69 | 10,490 kJ (2506 kcal) | 13,487 kJ (3221 kcal) | 14,986 kJ (3579 kcal) |
| | 70+ | 8931 kJ (2133 kcal) | 11,482 kJ (2742 kcal) | 12,758 kJ (3047 kcal) |

## CALCULATING YOUR DAILY REQUIREMENTS

### Energy needs

The number of calories or kilojoules you need per day to maintain or lose weight depends on many factors, including age, gender and levels of physical activity. Illness can also significantly affect energy requirements, especially prolonged fever or serious conditions such as cancer.

To determine your own energy needs more precisely, you can use an energy calculator, such as the one provided on the Australian Government's Eat for Health website (www. eatforhealth.gov.au/node/add/calculator-energy). Alternatively, you can use the table above (sourced from Eatforhealth website) as a general guide.

Pregnant women need to add 1400 kilojoules (330 kcal) per day in the second trimester and 1900 kilojoules (450 kcal) per day in the third trimester (no change is necessary for the first trimester). Women who are breastfeeding need to add 2000–2100 kilojoules (480–500 kcal) per day.

### Protein, fat and carbohydrate needs

Nutritionists refer to protein, fat and carbohydrate as macronutrients, because we eat them in 'macro' or large quantities relative to micronutrients such as vitamins and they all contribute to energy intake.

The macronutrient balance within our diets can have a significant impact on our health, and there has been a lot of research into high/low-protein, high/low-fat and high/low-carbohydrate diets. There is no one size fits all when it comes to ideal diets for the prevention and management of chronic disease. While a low-carbohydrate diet may be suitable for someone with diabetes, a high-protein diet is vital for someone who is undernourished and recovering from an acute illness.

The traditional Mediterranean diet varies a little across the different Mediterranean regions but is generally moderately low in protein (contributing 12–15 per cent of total energy), moderate in carbohydrate (40–45 per cent) and high in fat (35–40 per cent), and includes some alcohol (about 5 per cent).

The traditional Mediterranean diet falls well within health authority guidelines, at the lower end for protein and carbohydrate and at the higher end for fat (with a high proportion of healthy monounsaturated fats from olive oil, of course).

## Micronutrient needs

Micronutrients are the vitamins and minerals we need in very small amounts. The table on the right shows the average daily micronutrient requirements for a 40-year-old woman or man.

The recommended daily intake (RDI) is the amount that is sufficient to meet the nutrient needs of nearly all healthy individuals. In fact, only 5–10 per cent of the population will have requirements this high; most of us will need no more than half this amount. If your intake is a little bit less than the listed values, this should not mean you're deficient. If your intake is consistently about half the RDI, then you may be at risk of deficiency in the long term.

## Recommended daily intakes of micronutrients

| NUTRIENT | DAILY REQUIREMENT | |
| --- | --- | --- |
| | Women (aged 40) | Men (aged 40) |
| Omega-3 fats* | 90 mg | 160 mg |
| Fibre | 25 g | 30 g |
| Vitamin A | 700 µg | 900 µg |
| Thiamine (vitamin B1) | 1.1 mg | 1.2 mg |
| Riboflavin (vitamin B2) | 1.1 mg | 1.3 mg |
| Niacin (vitamin B3) | 14 mg | 16 mg |
| Vitamin B6 | 1.3 mg | 1.3 mg |
| Vitamin B12 | 2.4 µg | 2.4 µg |
| Folate/folic acid (vitamin B9) | 400 µg | 400 µg |
| Vitamin C | 45 mg | 45 mg |
| Calcium | 1000 mg | 1000 mg |
| Iodine | 150 µg | 150 µg |
| Iron | 18 mg | 8 mg |
| Magnesium | 320 mg | 420 mg |
| Potassium | 2800 mg | 3800 mg |
| Sodium | 460–920 mg | 460–920 mg |
| Zinc | 8 mg | 14 mg |

*Source: eatforhealth.gov.au*
*\*The long-chain omega-3 fats are eicosapentaenoic acid (EPA), docosahexaenoic acid (DHA) and docosapentaenoic acid (DPA), which are only available in animal foods or supplements. For prevention of chronic disease, the government recommends intakes of up to 400 mg per day. For people who have experienced a heart attack, the National Heart Foundation recommends an intake of 1 gram EPA+DHA per day, and two serves of oily fish per week.*

# Fasting Menu

| DAY | BREAKFAST | LUNCH | DINNER | SNACKS |
|---|---|---|---|---|
| **SUNDAY** | Greek Fritatta (page 114) | Fish Soup (page 165) Slice sourdough bread (page 46) | Deconstructed Moussaka (page 150) Northern Greek Salad (page 98) | Greek-style yoghurt with 1 teaspoon honey and sprinkle of cinnamon Pear and bunch grapes Hazelnuts (8–10) |
| **MONDAY** | Boiled/poached egg, fresh ricotta and tomato on sourdough bread sprinkled with herbs and olive oil (page 50) | Tomato Fritters (page 66) with hummus (page 58) and Coral Lettuce Salad (page 101) | Pea and Artichoke Casserole with Pork (page 132) Rocket Salad | Chewy Almond Biscuit (page 178) Slice of watermelon Apple Greek-style yoghurt Walnuts (5) and dried apricots (4–5) |
| **TUESDAY** | Sliced avocado on sourdough bread drizzled with olive oil, balsamic and crumbled goat's feta | Prawn and Black-eyed Bean Salad (page 106) Slice sourdough bread (page 46) | Pearl Barley Risotto made with zucchini, sweet potato, spinach and crumbled feta Tossed green salad | Greek-style yoghurt with berries Pear and orange Almonds (8–10) Hazelnut Biscotti (page 191) |
| **WEDNESDAY (Fasting Day)** | Chopped tomato, red onion, cucumber and herbs on rye crispbread drizzled with balsamic glaze and 1 teaspoon olive oil | Maria's Sardinian Minestrone (page 90) with rye crispbread | Prawns Saganaki (no cheese) (page 162). Green salad made with cos lettuce, vinegar, 1 teaspoon olive oil, balsamic vinegar, herbs | Herbal teas Orange |
| **THURSDAY** | Boiled egg, fresh ricotta and tomato on sourdough bread sprinkled with herbs and olive oil (page 50) | Stuffed Tomatoes with Pine Nuts and Currants (page 76) Mediterranean Salad (page 97) | Grilled Chicken Skewers on Sicilian Caponata (page 142) | Poached apples with yoghurt and cinnamon Walnuts and dates Bunch grapes |
| **FRIDAY (Fasting Day)** | Tablespoon of Smoky Eggplant, Roasted Peanut and Feta Dip (page 58) on rye crispbread topped with sliced cucumber and tomato | Maria's Sardinian Minestrone (page 90) with barley rusk (paximadi) or rye crispbread | Lamb salad (100 g grilled lamb fillet, 1 cup chopped cos lettuce, 6 halved cherry tomatoes, ½ sliced red onion, ½ Lebanese cucumber, dressed with fresh lemon juice and herbs) | Herbal teas Apple |
| **SATURDAY** | Cooked cereal (porridge or semolina) with sliced banana and cinnamon | Tiana and Adam's Paella (page 128) Coral Lettuce Salad (page 101) | Slow-cooked Beef Cheek and Eggplant Casserole (page 136) on Cauliflower and Bean Purée (page 60) Northern Greek Salad (page 98) | Baked Custard Pie with Filo Pastry (page 186) Watermelon and mandarin Almonds and apricots |

*Menu provides the following energy = 8500 kJ on non-fasting days and 2500 kJ on fasting days = 7000 kJ on average (20% less than energy requirements of average female with sedentary lifestyle). Protein 17%, Fat 42%, Carbohydrates 34%, Fibre 29 g. Adequate in all nutrients expect for calcium. Suggest this is followed for maximum of 3 months for weight loss.*

# Vegetarian Menu Lacto-ovo

| DAY | BREAKFAST | LUNCH | DINNER | SNACKS |
|---|---|---|---|---|
| SUNDAY | Boiled/poached egg, fresh ricotta and tomato on sourdough bread sprinkled with herbs and olive oil (page 50) | Pearl Barley Risotto with Eggplant, Pumpkin, Sundried Tomatoes, Basil and Feta (page 83) Coral Lettuce Salad (page 101) | Vegetarian Cabbage Rolls (page 121) Baby Cos, Radicchio and Fennel Salad | Greek-style yoghurt with 1 teaspoon honey and sprinkle of cinnamon Orange and 1 slice honeydew melon Chewy fruit and nut bars |
| MONDAY | Cooked cereal (porridge or semolina) with sliced banana and cinnamon | Chick Pea Fritters (page 72) with Spicy Feta Dip Northern Greek Salad (page 98) | Pastry-less Spanakopita (page 80) Mediterranean Salad (page 97) | Greek-style yoghurt with berries Bunch grapes and 1 pear Slice of Yoghurt Cake (page 190) Hazelnuts (8–10) |
| TUESDAY | Sliced avocado on sourdough bread drizzled with olive oil, balsamic and crumbled goat's feta | Chick Pea and Spinach Soup (page 94) Slice sourdough bread (page 46) | Pearl Barley Risotto made with zucchini, sweet potato, spinach and crumbled feta Tossed green salad | Greek-style yoghurt with poached pears Walnuts (5) and dates (3–4) Hazelnut Biscotti (page 191) Herbal tea or Greek coffee/ espresso |
| WEDNESDAY | Greek-style yoghurt with fresh berries and crushed walnuts | Rainbow Silverbeet with Rice (page 117) Slice sourdough bread (page 46) | Greek Frittata (page 114) Baby Cos, Radicchio and Fennel Salad | Slice of Chestnut, Almond and Fig Cake (page 193) Almonds (8–10) Dried apricots (2–3) Mandarin and fresh figs |
| THURSDAY | Boiled/poached egg, fresh ricotta and tomato on sourdough bread sprinkled with herbs and olive oil (page 50) | Tomato Fritters (page 66) with hummus (page 58) Coral Lettuce Salad (page 101) | Vegetable and Lentil Soup (page 93) Spinach, Fig and Anthotiro Salad (page 105) | Baked Quince with yoghurt (page 197) Walnuts (5) Bunch grapes and 1 slice watermelon |
| FRIDAY | Cooked cereal (porridge or semolina) with sliced banana and cinnamon | Cavolo Nero with Borlotti Beans (page 118) Slice sourdough bread (page 46) | Spicy Greek Bean Medley (page 113) Greek Slaw (page 109) | Chewy Almond Biscuits (page 178) Greek-style yoghurt with crushed walnuts and honey Apple and pear |
| SATURDAY | Greek Frittata (page 114) | Eggplant Parmigiana (page 79) Mediterranean Salad (page 97) | Stuffed Tomatoes with Pine Nuts and Currants (page 76) Greek Slaw (page 109) | Greek Doughnuts with scoop ice cream and sprinkle of cinnamon (page 189) Mandarin and bunch grapes Hazelnuts (8–10) |

*Menu provides the following energy for weight maintenance: 8300-8500 kj*
*Protein 12%, Fat 45% (>50% monounsaturated), Carbohydrates 40%, Fibre 36 g. High in folate, vitamin C, fibre, beta-carotene equivalents.*

# Traditional Mediterranenan Festive Menu

| DAY | BREAKFAST | LUNCH | DINNER | SNACKS |
|---|---|---|---|---|
| SUNDAY | Boiled/poached egg, fresh ricotta and tomato on sourdough bread sprinkled with herbs and olive oil (page 50) Greek coffee/espresso | Baked Red Mullet (page 169) with steamed broccoli dressed with olive oil and fresh lemon juice | Greek Dim Sims (Lahanodolmades) (page 133) Baby Cos, Radicchio and Fennel Salad | Greek-style yoghurt with 1 teaspoon honey and sprinkle of cinnamon Wedge of honeydew melon 2 tablespoons pumpkin seeds (in shell) Herbal tea |
| MONDAY | Wedge of rockmelon with 2 slices prosciutto and 1 slice mozzarella cheese Greek coffee/espresso | Eggplant Parmigiana (page 79) Tossed green salad | Maria's Sardinian Minestrone (page 90) Sourdough bread (page 46) Olives and thin slice provolone cheese | Greek-style yoghurt with 1 tablespoon crushed hazelnuts Pear and bunch grapes Slice of Yoghurt Cake (page 190) Dried broad beans |
| TUESDAY | Sliced avocado on sourdough bread drizzled with olive oil, balsamic and crumbled goat's feta Greek coffee/espresso | Vegetable and Lentil Soup (page 93) with 1 wedge of Cheesy Polenta Bread (page 54) | Beef Stifado served with rice (page 140) Coral Lettuce Salad (page 83) Glass of red wine | Greek-style yoghurt with poached pears Walnuts (5) and dates (3–4) Hazelnut Biscotti (page 191) Herbal tea or Greek coffee/ espresso |
| WEDNESDAY | Greek-style yoghurt with fresh berries and flaked almonds | Rainbow Silverbeet with rice (page 117) | Chicken Saganaki (page 153) Northern Greek Salad (page 98) | Slice of Chestnut, Almond and Fig Cake (page 193) Dried chick peas and sultanas snack Stone fruits (apricot, plum) Figs Stuffed with Ricotta, Honey and Walnuts |
| THURSDAY | Boiled/poached egg, fresh ricotta and tomato on sourdough bread sprinkled with herbs and olive oil (page 50) | Open Lamb Souvlaki with Spicy Tzatziki (page 144) Northern Greek Salad (page 98) | Marinated chargrilled Quail (page 63) with Baby Cos, Radicchio and Fennel Salad Glass red wine | Baked Quince with yoghurt (page 197) Walnuts (4–5 whole in shell) Bunch grapes and 1 slice watermelon |
| FRIDAY | Marinated sardines with sliced cherry tomatoes and fresh herbs on sourdough toast (page 46) Greek coffee espresso | Cavolo Nero with Borlotti Beans (page 118) Slice sourdough bread (page 46) | Calamari With Salad of Wild Greens (page 161) Slice sourdough bread (page 46) | Chewy Almond Biscuits (page 178) Greek-style yoghurt with crushed walnuts and honey Apple and pear |
| SATURDAY | Fresh figs (2–3) or 1 wedge rockmelon with 1–2 slices prosciutto and 1 slice mozzarella cheese Greek coffee/espresso | Whole Mussels with Rice (page 170) Coral Lettuce Salad (page 83) Slice sourdough bread (page 46) | Slow-roasted Goat (page 149) with Slow-baked Root Vegetables in Honey and Balsamic Glaze (page 75) Greek Slaw (page 109) | Greek Doughuts with scoop ice cream and sprinkle of cinnamon (page 189) Mandarin and bunch grapes Dried broadbeans |

*Modified traditional menu. Menu provides approximately 8800 kJ (2100 kcal) in energy: Protein 17%, Fat 41% (>50% Monunsaturated), Carbohydrates 36%, Fibre 36g. High in folate, Vitamin C, fibre, b-carotene equivalents, amnd long chain omega-3 fats.*

Part Two

# Traditional Mediterranean Recipes

# Breakfast and Snacks

## Po Proino

# Sourdough Bread
## Horiatiko psomi me prozimi

### SOUR YEAST MIXTURE (PROZIMI)

½ cup (125 ml) lukewarm water

60 g fresh yeast, crumbled or 1½ tablespoons
(3 × 7 g sachets) dried yeast

½ cup (75 g) bread flour

### BREAD

2½ cups (625 ml) lukewarm water

1 quantity sour yeast mixture (see above)

1 kg bread flour, plus extra for dusting

1 teaspoon salt

3 tablespoons (45 ml) olive oil

**NUTRIENT COMPOSITION PER 60 G SERVE**
(1 large continental slice or 2 thin slices):

|  | Quantity per serve | %RDI ♀ | %RDI ♂ |
|---|---|---|---|
| Energy | 595 kJ (142 kcal) | 7 | 6 |
| Protein | 4.1 g | 6 | 5 |
| Carbohydrate | 26.0 g | 11 | 9 |
| Total fat | 2.3 g | 3 | 2 |
| Saturated fat | 0.4 g | 3 | 1 |
| Sodium | 80 mg* | 5 | 5 |
| Fibre | 1.5 g** | 6 | 5 |

\* This bread is low in salt.
** You can boost the fibre content by using a mixture
of rye flour and wholemeal flour.

You'll have to think ahead with this recipe, as the sour yeast mixture needs to stand overnight before use. The yeast will multiply and consume the flour, creating a sour mixture that will give the bread its characteristic flavour and dense texture.

**1**  The night before you want to make the bread, prepare the sour yeast mixture. Pour lukewarm water into a large bowl (in case the culture rises a lot) and stir in yeast. Add flour, mix well, then cover and set aside overnight.

**2**  The next morning, make the bread. Gradually stir lukewarm water into sour yeast mixture, then gradually stir in flour until well combined. Incorporate salt and olive oil, then turn dough out onto a floured bench top and knead until smooth. Dust dough with flour, then return to bowl, cover and set aside in a warm place to prove for 1 hour, or until doubled in size.

**3**  Grease and flour 2 loaf tins or line them with baking paper.

**4**  Cut dough into 2 pieces, shape into loaves and drop into prepared loaf tins.

**5**  Leave to prove in a warm area for about 1 hour, or until doubled in size.

**6**  Meanwhile, preheat oven to 180°C.

**7**  Bake loaves for 60 minutes, or until bread is golden brown and sounds hollow when tapped on the bottom.

**MAKES TWO LOAVES**

# *Making Yoghurt*
## *Spitiko yiaourti*

**4 cups (1 litre) full-cream milk**

**100 g natural yoghurt (with live cultures)**

| NUTRIENT COMPOSITION PER 200 G (190 ML) SERVE: | | | |
|---|---|---|---|
| | Average quantity per serving | %RDI ♀ | %RDI ♂ |
| Energy | 588 kJ (117 kcal) | 7 | 6 |
| Protein | 6.8 g | 9 | 7 |
| Carbohydrate | 12 g | 5 | 4 |
| Total fat | 7.5 g | 8 | 7 |
| Saturated fat | 4.8 g | 34 | 17 |
| Sodium | 76 mg | 5 | 5 |
| Fibre | 0 | 0 | 0 |
| Calcium | 199 mg | 20 | 20 |

You will need a heavy-based pot (or double-boiler), a thermometer and an insulated storage pot (ideally a yoghurt-maker, but you could also use a thermos, or any lidded container wrapped in a warm towel or blanket).

You can flavour your yoghurt with fresh fruit and nuts, for example: blueberries and sliced almonds, sliced banana and crushed walnuts, honey and crushed walnuts, or crushed hazelnuts and sliced apricots or peaches.

**1** Slowly heat milk in a heavy-based saucepan over medium heat until it reaches 90–95°C. Remove from heat and cool down quickly to 35–40°C (you can put the saucepan in an ice bath to do this, but keep an eye on it).

**2** Whisk in yoghurt.

**3** Pour mixture into insulated storage pot and store at a warm temperature for 8 hours, or until yoghurt sets. If you are using an insulated pot (as many yoghurt makers have) it will be fine on the kitchen bench. Otherwise wrap the pot or jar with a warm blanket and place away from a draught.

**4** Refrigerate and use as required.

---

**TOPPING IDEAS FOR A HEALTHY BREAKFAST OR SNACK:**

* *Crushed walnuts and honey*
* *Flaked almonds, blueberries and cinnamon*
* *Crushed hazelnuts, sliced fresh figs or chopped dried figs and nutmeg*
* *Linseed meal, sliced banana and cinnamon*
* *Diced fresh fruit salad with trickle of maple syrup*
* *Fresh sliced strawberries and balsamic glaze*

# Simple Mediterranean Breakfast *a la Roma*

50 g fresh ricotta

1 slice sourdough rye bread, toasted

2 eggs, boiled or poached

2–3 wedges fresh Roma tomato

1–2 teaspoons olive oil

freshly milled sea salt, to taste

freshly ground black pepper, to taste

SERVES 1

A simple breakfast commonly enjoyed by Romans during the summer months when tomatoes are a rich red colour and full of flavour.

Spread the ricotta on the rye bread and top with eggs. Sit tomatoes alongside and drizzle with olive oil. Season with salt and pepper, and serve.

**NUTRIENT COMPOSITION PER 220 G SERVE:**

|  | Average quantity per serving | %RDI ♀ | %RDI ♂ |
|---|---|---|---|
| Energy | 1780 kJ (425 kcal) | 22 | 17 |
| Protein | 22.2 g | 31 | 25 |
| Carbohydrate | 22.0 g | 10 | 8 |
| Total fat | 27.8 g | 31 | 32 |
| Saturated fat | 8.7 g | 62 | 31 |
| Sodium | 357 mg | 22 | 22 |
| Fibre | 2.4 g | 10 | 8 |

# Vegetarian Breakfast with Smashed Avocado *Frigania me avokanto kai feta*

½ ripe avocado

30 g marinated goat's cheese

1 slice sourdough rye bread, toasted

juice of ½ lemon

2 teaspoons olive oil

1 cup (80 g) small button mushrooms

1 teaspoon dry or chopped fresh mixed herbs

½ clove garlic, crushed

1 Roma tomato, cut into quarters

freshly ground black pepper, to taste

freshly milled sea salt, to taste

SERVES 1

**Every morning my younger daughter Vivienne can be found in the kitchen mashing up avocado, mixing through goat's cheese and carefully spreading on wholegrain toast and then decorating with an artistic display of balsamic glaze. This breakfast makes her feel good and focus on study, she says!**

1  Mash avocado flesh with a fork in a small bowl. Mix through goat's cheese, spread on toasted bread, and sprinkle with lemon juice.

2  Heat half the olive oil in a frying pan over medium heat, then lightly sauté mushrooms. Sprinkle with half the herbs and garlic. Remove from the pan.

3  Heat remaining olive oil in the same pan over medium heat. Sprinkle the tomato quarters with remaining garlic and herbs, and lightly sear in hot pan.

4  Serve the mushrooms and tomatoes on the avocado toast. Season to taste.

**NUTRIENT COMPOSITION PER SERVE:**

|  | Average quantity per serving | %RDI ♀ | %RDI ♂ |
|---|---|---|---|
| Energy | 1796 kJ (429 kcal) | 22 | 18 |
| Protein | 17.1 g | 24 | 19 |
| Carbohydrate | 25.3 g | 11 | 9 |
| Total fat | 28.9 g | 32 | 26 |
| Saturated fat | 9.0 g | 64 | 32 |
| Sodium | 332 mg | 21 | 21 |
| Fibre | 8.9 g | 36 | 30 |

Simple Mediterranean Breakfast

Roasted Whisky Peanuts

# Roasted Whisky Peanuts *Fistikia me ouiski*

3 cups (500 g) raw peanuts, skin on

½ cup (125 ml) whisky or cognac

½ cup (125 g) coarse salt

You can also cover the peanuts in a mixture of flour and salt, which creates a crispy edible salty shell.

1 Preheat oven to 180°C.

2 Spread peanuts in a roasting tray. Pour whisky over peanuts and ensure they're coated well. Sprinkle salt over peanuts, coating well.

3 Roast for 15–20 minutes, or until peanuts are golden.

NUTRIENT COMPOSITION PER 2 TABLESPOON (30 G) SERVE:

| | Average quantity per serving | %RDI ♀ | ♂ |
|---|---|---|---|
| Energy | 847 kJ (202 kcal) | 10 | 8 |
| Protein | 8.2 g | 11 | 9 |
| Carbohydrate | 3.4 g | 2 | 1 |
| Total fat | 15.7 g | 17 | 14 |
| Saturated fat | 2.4 g | 17 | 9 |
| Sodium | 1000 mg* | 63 | 63 |
| Fibre | 2.7 g | 11 | 9 |

*Without coating, the salt level of peanuts is very low (less than 1 mg).*

---

# Greco-Mexican Corn on the Cob with Feta and Chilli *Kalamboki sta karvouna me feta*

6 corn cobs

1½ tablespoons olive oil or 30 g butter, melted

60 g feta cheese, crumbled

½ teaspoon chilli powder

freshly milled sea salt, to taste

freshly ground black pepper, to taste

1 lime, cut into wedges

A variation on the popular Mexican barbecued corn, but with a Greek touch – feta instead of Mexican cotija cheese.

1 Heat a barbecue or chargrill pan and grill corn, turning regularly, until kernels are cooked and slightly charred.

2 Drizzle over olive oil or butter, sprinkle with feta and chilli powder, and season with salt and pepper.

3 Serve with lime wedges to squeeze over.

SERVES 6

NUTRIENT COMPOSITION PER SERVE:

| | Average quantity per serving | %RDI ♀ | ♂ |
|---|---|---|---|
| Energy | 835 kJ (199 kcal) | 10 | 8 |
| Protein | 7.8 g | 11 | 9 |
| Carbohydrate | 19.6 g | 9 | 7 |
| Total fat | 9.8 g | 11 | 9 |
| Saturated fat | 2.5 g | 9 | 9 |
| Sodium | 117 mg | 7 | 7 |
| Fibre | 8.8 g* | 35 | 29 |

*This dish is high in fibre.*

# Cheesy Polenta Bread
## Kalambokisio Tiropsomo

3 cups (750 ml) milk

1 cup (180 g) fine polenta

1 teaspoon baking powder

3 eggs, lightly beaten

200 g kefalograviera cheese, grated

½ teaspoon freshly ground black pepper

200 g feta cheese, crumbled

2 tablespoons sliced olives

handful fresh basil leaves, for garnish

A rich creamy bread that can be enjoyed by people avoiding gluten. Some people also top the bread with sundried tomatoes. Serve as a side dish with salads, soups or casseroles, or enjoy on its own as a snack.

**1** Preheat oven to 180°C and grease a loaf tin.

**2** Heat milk in a saucepan over medium heat until hot but not boiling. Add polenta and baking powder, then whisk for 10 minutes, or until polenta starts to thicken. Remove from heat.

**3** Slowly pour in eggs while continuing to whisk. Stir through kefalograviera and pepper. Pour into prepared tin or pie dish and sprinkle over feta. Top with sliced olives.

**4** Bake for 35 minutes, or until cooked through and golden brown on top. Allow to cool slightly before cutting and serving. Garnish with basil.

**SERVES 8**

### NUTRIENT COMPOSITION PER SERVE:

| | Average quantity per serving | %RDI ♀ | %RDI ♂ |
|---|---|---|---|
| Energy | 1685 kJ (402 kcal) | 20 | 16 |
| Protein | 16.1 g | 22 | 18 |
| Carbohydrate | 20.6 g | 9 | 7 |
| Total fat | 28.6 g | 32 | 26 |
| Saturated fat | 13.4 g | 96 | 48 |
| Sodium | 857 mg | 54 | 54 |
| Fibre | 1.1 g | 4 | 4 |

### LOW-FAT VERSION
(replace milk and cheeses with low-fat options):

| | Average quantity per serving | %RDI ♀ | %RDI ♂ |
|---|---|---|---|
| Energy | 1407 kJ (336 kcal) | 17 | 14 |
| Protein | 22.2 g | 31 | 25 |
| Carbohydrate | 19.8 g | 9 | 7 |
| Total fat | 18.7 g | 21 | 17 |
| Saturated fat | 7.4 g | 53 | 26 |
| Sodium | 643 mg | 40 | 40 |
| Fibre | 0.8 g | 3 | 3 |

# Dips and Mezedes

## Orektika

# Chick Pea and Tahini Dip  *Hummus*

1 × 440 g can chick peas, drained

⅓ cup (80 ml) tahini

¼ cup (60 ml) olive oil

1 small clove garlic, peeled

½ cup (125 ml) water

¼ cup (60 ml) fresh lemon juice (or try half lemon, half lime juice)

½ teaspoon salt

½ teaspoon ground cumin

paprika, to garnish

chopped fresh flat-leaf parsley, to garnish

This is a perfect dip to make in a hurry when friends drop by, using ingredients from your pantry. Tahini paste can be bought from Mediterranean delicatessens and keeps for ages in the refrigerator.

**1** Blend all ingredients except the paprika and parsley in a food processor until smooth and creamy.

**2** Refrigerate until ready to eat. Sprinkle over paprika and garnish with parsley just before serving.

**NUTRIENT COMPOSITION PER 2 TABLESPOON (40 G) SERVE:**

| | Average quantity per serving | %RDI ♀ | %RDI ♂ |
|---|---|---|---|
| Energy | 280 kJ (67 kcal) | 3 | 3 |
| Protein | 2.1 g | 3 | 2 |
| Carbohydrate | 2.9 g | 1 | 1 |
| Total fat | 5.3 g | 6 | 5 |
| Saturated fat | 0.7 g | 5 | 3 |
| Sodium | 118 mg | 7 | 7 |
| Fibre | 1.6 g | 6 | 5 |

# Smoky Eggplant, Roasted Peanut and Feta Dip  *Kapnisti melinzanosalata*

1 large eggplant

1 small clove garlic, crushed

2 tablespoons peanuts, toasted in a dry frying pan

1 tablespoon olive oil

50 g feta cheese, crumbled

1 tablespoon chopped fresh flat-leaf parsley

freshly milled sea salt, to taste

freshly ground black pepper, to taste

Dietitian/Chef Sharon Croxford cooks the whole eggplant on the naked flame of a gas stove which chars the skin to get that Eastern Mediterranean flavour.

**1** Sit eggplant on gas stovetop directly over a low flame and roast for about 5 minutes, turning frequently with tongs, until skin is charred and flesh is soft. If you don't have a gas stovetop, you can cook the eggplant under a hot grill, turning to ensure even cooking.

**2** Remove eggplant from heat and allow to cool, then carefully remove and discard charred skin.

**3** Blend eggplant flesh, garlic, peanuts and olive oil in food processor and process to a rough consistency using the pulse setting.

**4** Using a spoon, stir in feta, parsley, salt and pepper. Serve immediately.

**NUTRIENT COMPOSITION PER 2 TABLESPOON (40 G) SERVE:**

| | Average quantity per serving | %RDI ♀ | %RDI ♂ |
|---|---|---|---|
| Energy | 195 kJ (47 kcal) | 2 | 2 |
| Protein | 1.7 g | 2 | 2 |
| Carbohydrate | 1.1 g | 1 | 1 |
| Total fat | 3.9 g | 4 | 4 |
| Saturated fat | 1.0 g | 8 | 4 |
| Sodium | 48 mg | 3 | 3 |
| Fibre | 1.2 g | 5 | 4 |

*Spicy Feta Dip*
(see page 60)

*Chick Pea
and Tahini Dip*

*Smoky Eggplant,
Roasted Peanut
and Feta Dip*

# Spicy Feta Dip *Tirokafteri*

250 g feta cheese

1 tablespoon olive oil

1 tablespoon white wine vinegar

1 small red chilli, deseeded and finely chopped

1 Purée all the ingredients in a food processor until creamy.

2 Serve with crusty bread or crackers.

**NUTRIENT COMPOSITION PER 1½ TABLESPOON (30 G) SERVE:**

| | Average quantity per serving | %RDI ♀ | %RDI ♂ |
|---|---|---|---|
| Energy | 361 kJ (86 kcal) | 4 | 4 |
| Protein | 4.3 g | 6 | 5 |
| Carbohydrate | 0.1 g | 0 | 0 |
| Total fat | 7.5 g | 8 | 7 |
| Saturated fat | 4.0 g | 29 | 14 |
| Sodium | 276 mg | 17 | 17 |
| Fibre | 0.2 g | 1 | 1 |

# Cauliflower and Bean Purée
## Poures me kounoupidi kai fassolia

300 g cauliflower, roughly chopped and steamed

1 × 440 g can cannellini beans, drained

2 tablespoons olive oil

1 clove garlic, crushed

¼ teaspoon salt

freshly ground black pepper, to taste

**This can be served as a base for meatballs or fried fish, or eaten as a dip.**

Purée all the ingredients in a food processor until creamy.

**NUTRIENT COMPOSITION PER 4–5 TABLESPOON (100 G) SERVE:**

| | Average quantity per serving | %RDI ♀ | %RDI ♂ |
|---|---|---|---|
| Energy | 309 kJ (74 kcal) | 4 | 3 |
| Protein | 2.0 g | 3 | 2 |
| Carbohydrate | 2.4 g | 1 | 1 |
| Total fat | 6.3 g | 7 | 6 |
| Saturated fat | 1.0 g | 7 | 4 |
| Sodium | 124 mg | 8 | 8 |
| Fibre | 2.8 g | 11 | 10 |

Cauliflower and Bean Purée

# Roasted Feta with Red Capsicum Purée
## Feta psiti me piperies

This creamy feta in a puréed bed of capsicum is perfect served with crusty bread and a glass of wine.

2 red capsicums

1 clove garlic, crushed

2 tablespoons olive oil

⅓ cup (35 g) walnuts, crushed or finely chopped

freshly milled sea salt, to taste

freshly ground black pepper, to taste

200 g feta cheese

1 Preheat oven to 220°C and line baking tray with baking paper.

2 Place capsicums on prepared baking tray and roast for 30 minutes, or until they soften and the skin blisters. Remove from oven and turn heat down to 180°C.

3 Allow capsicums to cool, then peel off and discard skin. Deseed capsicums then purée with garlic and olive oil in a food processor.

4 Line a small baking dish with larger piece of foil (so it hangs over the sides) and pour the puréed capsicum on top. Sprinkle over walnuts, and season with salt and pepper. Place feta (in one piece) in the centre of capsicum purée and fold over foil to make a parcel.

5 Bake for 20 minutes, or until feta is roasted and creamy. Serve immediately as a mezze or as an accompaniment to other dishes.

**NUTRIENT COMPOSITION PER 2–3 TABLESPOON (50 G) SERVE:**

| | Average quantity per serving | %RDI ♀ | ♂ |
|---|---|---|---|
| Energy | 338 kJ (81 kcal) | 4 | 3 |
| Protein | 3.2 g | 4 | 4 |
| Carbohydrate | 1.5 g | 1 | 1 |
| Total fat | 7.0 g | 8 | 6 |
| Saturated fat | 2.4 g | 17 | 8 |
| Sodium | 139 mg | 9 | 9 |
| Fibre | 0.9 g | 4 | 3 |

# Spicy Yoghurt and Cucumber Dip   Tzatziki Kaftero

1 small Lebanese cucumber, peeled and grated

1 clove garlic, finely chopped

1–2 tablespoons fresh dill, finely chopped

250 g thick Greek-style yoghurt

1 tablespoon olive oil

1 tablespoon white wine vinegar

¼ teaspoon cayenne pepper (or finely sliced fresh chilli)

freshly milled sea salt, to taste

freshly ground black pepper, to taste

A variation on the traditional Greek tzatziki with a little bite. Perfect with lamb souvlaki skewers.

1 Squeeze any excess liquid out of grated cucumber then mix with garlic and dill in a bowl.

2 Stir through yoghurt, then add olive oil, vinegar and cayenne pepper, then season with salt and pepper.

3 Refrigerate until ready to eat.

**NUTRIENT COMPOSITION PER 2 TABLESPOON (40 G) SERVE:**

| | Average quantity per serving | %RDI ♀ | ♂ |
|---|---|---|---|
| Energy | 184 kJ (44 kcal) | 2 | 2 |
| Protein | 1.6 g | 2 | 2 |
| Carbohydrate | 2.4 g | 1 | 1 |
| Total fat | 3.0 g | 3 | 3 |
| Saturated fat | 1.7 g | 12 | 6 |
| Sodium | 144 mg | 9 | 9 |
| Fibre | 0.3 g | 1 | 1 |

# Marinated Chargrilled Quail
## Ortikia sta karvouna

8 quail

2 tablespoons olive oil

½ cup (125 ml) red wine

1 clove garlic, crushed

1 red onion, grated

2 tablespoons chopped fresh oregano and/or thyme

freshly milled sea salt, to taste

freshly ground black pepper, to taste

**RADICCHIO AND FENNEL SALAD**

1 radicchio, roughly chopped

1 small bulb fennel, thinly sliced

1 medium red onion, sliced into rings

2 tablespoons olive oil

2 tablespoons balsamic vinegar

freshly milled sea salt, to taste

freshly ground black pepper, to taste

People of the Mediterranean love to eat game meats and this is a favourite which can be easily and quickly prepared on a grill plate or included at a barbecue. Many elderly Mediterranean people (Greek or Italian) will breed quail in their backyard so they can enjoy fresh quail throughout the year.

Quail is often served just pink in restaurants, but Greeks prefer the birds well cooked, with a strong charcoal flavour.

**1** Wash quail and rub all over with olive oil.

**2** Combine wine, garlic, onion, fresh herbs, and salt and pepper, and pour over quail. Cover and marinate in the refrigerator for at least 2 hours.

**3** Meanwhile, start to prepare the salad by tossing together the radicchio, fennel and onion.

**4** Preheat a charcoal barbecue or under-stove grill.

**5** Basting frequently with the marinade to prevent drying out, cook quail for 5–10 minutes on each side, or until done to your liking. (Alternatively, preheat oven to 180°C and bake quail in marinade for 20–30 minutes.)

**6** Toss the salad with olive oil and vinegar, and season with salt and pepper. Serve with quail.

**SERVES 8**

**NUTRIENT COMPOSITION PER SERVE:**

|  | Average quantity per serving | %RDI ♀ | %RDI ♂ |
|---|---|---|---|
| Energy | 943 kJ (225 kcal) | 11.4 | 9.2 |
| Protein | 21.6 g | 30.1 | 24.1 |
| Carbohydrate | 1.6 g | 0.7 | 0.5 |
| Total fat | 13.8 g | 15.3 | 12.5 |
| Saturated fat | 3.2 g | 23.2 | 11.6 |
| Sodium | 49 mg | 3.1 | 3.1 |
| Fibre | 1.4 g | 5.9 | 4.9 |

# Feta in a Filo Pastry Crust
## Feta Krousta

**1 × 250 g block feta cheese**

**6 sheets filo pastry**

**2 tablespoons olive oil**

**¼ cup (60 ml) honey**

**2 tablespoons lemon juice**

**2 tablespoons sesame seeds, toasted in
  a dry frying pan**

### NUTRIENT COMPOSITION PER SERVE:

| | Average quantity per serving | %RDI ♀ | ♂ |
|---|---|---|---|
| Energy | 1173 kJ (280 kcal) | 14 | 11 |
| Protein | 8.0 g | 11 | 9 |
| Carbohydrate | 21.4 g | 9 | 7 |
| Total fat | 18.3 g | 20 | 17 |
| Saturated fat | 6.6 g | 47 | 24 |
| Sodium | 472 mg | 30 | 30 |
| Fibre | 0.7 g | 3 | 2 |

**This mezze is an impressive parcel of warm creamy feta with a sweet and crunchy crust.**

**1** Cut feta lengthways into 6 long rectangles.

**2** Take a sheet of filo, fold in half and lay on the bench top with a short end facing you. Place a feta block in the centre of that end. Fold in sides and wrap the feta until you reach the other end of the filo.

**3** Heat olive oil in a frying pan over medium heat and fry the feta parcels until lightly browned. Remove from pan and drain on kitchen paper.

**4** Meanwhile, heat honey in a small saucepan then stir in lemon juice. Remove from heat.

**5** Using a slotted spoon, dip feta parcels in honey until well coated. Sprinkle with sesame seeds and serve hot. The feta will stay soft and creamy until the parcels cool down.

**SERVES 6**

# Tomato Fritters
## Ntomatokeftedes

400 g cherry tomatoes

1 teaspoon salt

1 large red onion, grated

⅓ cup (50 g) maize flour

80 g feta cheese, crumbled

1 egg, lightly beaten

1 tablespoon finely chopped sundried tomatoes

2 tablespoons finely chopped fresh flat-leaf parsley

2 tablespoons mint, finely chopped

½ teaspoon dried chilli flakes

1 teaspoon dried oregano

freshly milled sea salt, to taste

freshly ground black pepper, to taste

2–3 tablespoons olive oil

**NUTRIENT COMPOSITION PER FRITTER:**

|  | Average quantity per serving | %RDI ♀ | %RDI ♂ |
|---|---|---|---|
| Energy | 265 kJ (63 kcal) | 3 | 3 |
| Protein | 1.3 g | 2 | 1 |
| Carbohydrate | 5.0 g | 2 | 2 |
| Total fat | 4.2 g | 5 | 4 |
| Saturated fat | 1.2 g | 8 | 4 |
| Sodium | 127 mg | 8 | 8 |
| Fibre | 0.6 g | 3 | 2 |

These fritters are a popular mezze all over Greece, but especially in Santorini, where they are made with the local cherry tomatoes, which are particularly rich in minerals. An abbot of the Capuchin monastery in Ano Syros (the Cyclades) brought the first cherry tomatoes to Greece in 1818 and by 1875 they were regularly cultivated. By the 1900s, 20,000 acres of tomatoes were regularly being harvested in Santorini. One variety of cherry tomato is now called the Santorini or Tomatina.

**1** Drape a muslin cloth inside a small bowl. Cut tomatoes in half and squash to extract pulp into bowl, discarding skin. Sprinkle pulp with salt, tie up the muslin cloth then hang it over the bowl or the sink and drain for 30 minutes to remove excess liquid. Retain drained pulp and discard liquid.

**2** Transfer tomato pulp to bowl and add onion, maize flour, feta, egg, sundried tomato, parsley, mint, chilli flakes and oregano, and season with salt and pepper.

**3** Heat olive oil in a frying pan over low–medium heat (keep heat moderately low to prevent fritters from spattering and burning). Working in batches, drop in tablespoons of tomato mixture and fry until golden. Remove from pan and drain on kitchen paper while cooking the next batch.

**4** Serve hot with Spicy Tzatziki Dip (page 144) and salad.

**MAKES APPROXIMATELY 20 FRITTERS**

# Chicken Meatballs
## Keftedakia me kotopoulo

1 onion, finely chopped

2 cloves garlic, crushed

1 whole chilli, deseeded (optional) and finely sliced

1 teaspoon mixed dried herbs

½ cup (15 g) finely chopped fresh flat-leaf parsley

500 g chicken mince

⅓ cup (55 g) breadcrumbs (or rice crumbs for gluten-free)

2 tablespoons olive oil, plus extra for drizzling

freshly milled sea salt, to taste

freshly ground black pepper, to taste

**SPICY SALTSA**

500g ripe tomatoes

1 small red onion

1 clove garlic

1 medium red chilli

1 tablespoon olive oil

1 tablespoon chopped fresh basil

salt and pepper to season

**Serve this dish with Spicy Tzatziki (see page 144)**

**1** Preheat oven to 180°C and grease a baking dish that has a lid.

**2** Combine all ingredients in a bowl, then cover and refrigerate for about 1 hour.

**3** Spread olive oil on your hands and roll golf-ball-sized pieces of the mixture into balls. Arrange in prepared dish and drizzle over a little extra olive oil.

**4** Cover and bake for 35 minutes.

**5** Make the Spicy Saltsa. In small baking tray roast tomatoes, red onion, garlic and red chilli for 20 minutes until charred. Peel and blend. Stir in the olive oil and basil. Add salt and pepper to season.

**SERVES 6 (MAKES ABOUT 20 LARGE MEATBALLS)**

**NUTRIENT COMPOSITION PER 40 G PIECE:**

|  | Average quantity per serving | %RDI ♀ | %RDI ♂ |
|---|---|---|---|
| Energy | 217 kJ (52 kcal) | 2.6 | 2.1 |
| Protein | 6.0 g | 8.4 | 6.7 |
| Carbohydrate | 1.7 g | 0.7 | 0.6 |
| Total fat | 2.3 g | 2.6 | 2.1 |
| Saturated fat | 0.4 g | 3.1 | 1.6 |
| Sodium | 25 mg | 1.6 | 1.6 |
| Fibre | 0.5 g | 2.0 | 1.6 |

**PARTY OPTION**

*Roll mixture into balls the size of a large marble and shallow-fry in olive oil until golden. Serve as finger food. Makes about 30 small meatballs.*

# Legumes, Vegetarian and Fasting Foods

## Ospria, Ladera kai Nistisima

# Chick Pea Fritters
## Revithokeftedes

500 g dried chick peas, soaked overnight
  in cold water

3 onions, finely chopped

2 tomatoes, cut into cubes

1 egg, lightly beaten

½ teaspoon ground cumin

2 tablespoons chopped fresh flat-leaf parsley

½ teaspoon dried oregano

2 tablespoons grated kefalograviera cheese

½ cup (50–60 g) plain flour

oil for shallow-frying

**This recipe doesn't work with canned chick peas. Dried ones are best and after the soak they purée up well.**

**1** Drain chick peas and whizz in a food processor until roughly chopped.

**2** Transfer chick peas to a large bowl and combine with onion, tomato, egg, cumin, parsley, oregano and cheese. Add flour and mix well.

**3** Heat oil in a frying pan over medium heat. Working in batches, fry tablespoons of mixture for 2–3 minutes on each side, or until golden. Remove from pan and drain on kitchen paper while cooking the next batch.

**4** Serve hot.

**MAKES ABOUT 30 MEDIUM-SIZED FRITTERS**

### NUTRIENT COMPOSITION PER 3-FRITTER SERVE:

| | Average quantity per serving | %RDI ♀ | %RDI ♂ |
|---|---|---|---|
| Energy | 589 kJ (141 kcal) | 10.5 | 8.4 |
| Protein | 4.1 g | 8.5 | 6.8 |
| Carbohydrate | 9.7 g | 6.2 | 4.9 |
| Total fat | 9.5 g | 15.6 | 12.7 |
| Saturated fat | 2.0 g | 21.1 | 10.5 |
| Sodium | 111 mg | 10.2 | 10.2 |
| Fibre | 2.6 g | 15.3 | 12.8 |

# Slow-baked Root Vegetables in Honey and Balsamic Glaze
## Pantremena lahanika sto fourno

5 small beetroot, roots and leaves trimmed

6–8 Dutch carrots, peeled

6–8 purple carrots, peeled

8–10 radishes, roots and leaves trimmed

5–6 chat potatoes, whole, unpeeled

5–6 small Desiree potatoes, whole, unpeeled

4–5 cloves garlic, whole, peeled

4–5 golden shallots, whole, peeled

1 cup (50 g) baby spinach leaves

⅓ cup (80 ml) olive oil

¼ cup (60 ml) balsamic vinegar

2 tablespoons honey

½ cup (125 ml) water

freshly milled sea salt, to taste

freshly ground black pepper, to taste

This colourful medley of baked vegetables with a sweet caramelised glaze is a favourite vegetarian dish at Ecco café in Melbourne. Recipe donated by my dear friend Peter Amiridis.

1 Preheat oven to 150°C.

2 Wrap beetroot in aluminium foil and arrange in a roasting tin with the other vegetables except the spinach leaves.

3 Pour over olive oil, vinegar, honey and water, season with salt and pepper, then bake for 1 hour.

4 Toss the spinach leaves through prior to serving.

SERVES 10

NUTRIENT COMPOSITION PER 200 G SERVE:

| | Average quantity per serving | %RDI ♀ | %RDI ♂ |
|---|---|---|---|
| Energy | 676 kJ (162 kcal) | 8.2 | 6.6 |
| Protein | 3.3 g | 4.6 | 3.7 |
| Carbohydrate | 19.6 g | 8.5 | 6.8 |
| Total fat | 7.7 g | 8.6 | 7.0 |
| Saturated fat | 1.2 g | 8.7 | 4.3 |
| Sodium | 52 mg | 3.2 | 3.2 |
| Fibre | 5.6 g | 22.2 | 18.5 |

# Stuffed Tomatoes with Pine Nuts and Currants

## Gemistes ntomates me koukounaria kai stafides

8 truss tomatoes

2 tablespoons olive oil, plus extra for drizzling

1 small onion, finely chopped

1 cup (200 g) rice

60 g pine nuts

60 g currants

dried mixed herbs, to taste

freshly milled sea salt, to taste

freshly ground black pepper, to taste

Stuffed vegetables are a favourite across the Mediterranean. The pine nuts in this dish add a lovely crunch and boost the protein content. This dish can be served hot or cold and leftovers make a great lunch.

**1** Preheat oven to 180°C and grease a baking dish.

**2** Carefully cut off tops of tomatoes and put to one side. Remove pulp with a spoon, reserving the pulp for the filling.

**3** Heat olive oil in a frying pan over medium heat and sauté onion. Add rice and cook for 5 minutes, stirring until well coated in oil and heated through.

**4** Add pine nuts, currants, herbs and tomato pulp, then season with salt and pepper. Cook for a further 5–10 minutes, or until rice is almost cooked, then set aside to cool.

**5** Carefully spoon filling into tomato shells and arrange in prepared dish, placing them close together to ensure they are tightly packed (to prevent tomatoes from splitting open and falling over). Replace the tops on the tomatoes.

**6** Drizzle over a little olive oil and bake for 40 minutes.

**7** Serve 2 tomatoes per person.

**SERVES 4**

### NUTRIENT COMPOSITION PER SERVE:

|  | Average quantity per serving | %RDI ♀ | %RDI ♂ |
|---|---|---|---|
| Energy | 1906 kJ (455 kcal) | 23.1 | 18.6 |
| Protein | 9.4 g | 13.1 | 10.5 |
| Carbohydrate | 59.3 g | 25.8 | 20.6 |
| Total fat | 19.8 g | 22.1 | 18.0 |
| Saturated fat | 2.1 g | 14.9 | 7.4 |
| Sodium | 41 mg | 2.6 | 2.6 |
| Fibre | 6.8 g | 27.4 | 22.8 |

# Rosy Calabro's Eggplant Parmigiana
## Parmigiana di melanzane

2 large eggplants or 3 small (about 1 kg)

salt

olive oil, for shallow-frying

½ cup (50 g) grated Grana Padano (Italian sharp parmesan-style cheese)

handful of fresh basil leaves

1 cup (125 g) grated mozzarella cheese

### SALTSA/SUGO

1 tablespoon olive oil

1 medium red onion, finely chopped

2 cloves garlic, crushed

1 × 440 g can diced tomatoes

1½ cups (375 ml) puréed tomato

2 cups (500 ml) water

1 teaspoon dried mixed herbs

1 small hot fresh chilli, finely sliced (optional)

4 tablespoons roughly chopped fresh basil (half in sauce and half between eggplant layers)

freshly milled sea salt, to taste

freshly ground black pepper, to taste

A favourite Italian vegetarian dish enjoyed with a Caprese Salad (see page 109) and slice of sourdough bread. This recipe is one of Rosy Calabro's family favourites. When I cook this for my Greek family, I alternate with a layer of potato which mops up the sauce, is more filling and of course starts to resemble moussaka!

1  Preheat oven to 180°C and grease a large baking dish.

2  To make the saltsa, heat olive oil in a frying pan over medium heat and sauté onion until translucent. Add garlic and sauté for a further few minutes. Add diced tomato and puréed tomato, water, dried herbs and chilli (if using), then simmer for 20 minutes. Stir through fresh basil.

3  Meanwhile, slice eggplants lengthways, sprinkle all over with salt and leave in a colander for 20 minutes. Rinse under cold running water and dry on kitchen paper.

4  Heat olive oil in a frying pan over medium heat and fry eggplant until soft but not browned. Drain on kitchen paper.

5  Arrange a layer of eggplant over bottom of prepared dish, spread over a little prepared saltsa, a sprinkle of Grana Padano, and a sprinkle of basil leaves. Repeat until eggplant is used up, finishing with a layer of sauce topped with mozzarella.

6  Bake for 20 minutes. Allow to cool for 10 minutes before cutting and serving.

**SERVES 6**

**NUTRIENT COMPOSITION PER SERVE:**

|  | Average quantity per serving | %RDI ♀ | ♂ |
|---|---|---|---|
| Energy | 1332 kJ (318 kcal) | 16.2 | 13.0 |
| Protein | 15.3 g | 21.3 | 17.0 |
| Carbohydrate | 10.2 g | 4.4 | 3.5 |
| Total fat | 24.1 g | 26.8 | 21.9 |
| Saturated fat | 8.5 g | 60.8 | 30.4 |
| Sodium | 432 mg | 27.0 | 27.0 |
| Fibre | 7.0 g | 28.0 | 23.3 |

# Pastry-less Spanakopita with Mixed Greens
## Spanakopita horis fillo

⅓ cup (80 ml) extra virgin olive oil

1 onion, finely chopped

150 g silverbeet, finely chopped

150 g mixed wild greens (chicory, rocket, spinach, amaranth, stinging nettle)

freshly milled sea salt, to taste

freshly ground black pepper, to taste

80 g feta cheese, crumbled

4 eggs, lightly beaten

Markos Dymiotis combines freshly picked wild greens with fresh eggs to make this delightful vegetarian dish.

1 Preheat oven to 180°C and grease a flan dish.

2 Heat olive oil in a large saucepan over medium heat and sauté onion until translucent. Add greens and stir until wilted. Season with salt and pepper.

3 Transfer greens to prepared dish and sprinkle over feta. Pour over eggs.

4 Bake for 20 minutes, or until egg is cooked through and lightly browned.

SERVES 4

| NUTRIENT COMPOSITION PER SERVE: | | | |
|---|---|---|---|
| | Average quantity per serving | %RDI ♀ | ♂ |
| Energy | 1189 kJ (284 kcal) | 14.4 | 11.6 |
| Protein | 10.8 g | 15.1 | 12.1 |
| Carbohydrate | 2.3 g | 1.0 | 0.8 |
| Total fat | 26.0 g | 28.9 | 23.6 |
| Saturated fat | 7.1 g | 50.9 | 25.5 |
| Sodium | 376 mg | 23.5 | 23.5 |
| Fibre | 2.1 g | 8.1 | 6.7 |

# Baked Pumpkin with Spices and Yoghurt
## Kolokithi sto fourno me yiaourti

1 × 1–1.5 kg wedge pumpkin (Jap or Kent), skin on, sliced into thick wedges

½ teaspoon ground cinnamon

½ teaspoon mixed spice

freshly milled sea salt, to taste

freshly ground black pepper, to taste

⅓ cup (80 ml) olive oil

⅓ cup (80 ml) honey

⅓ cup (80 ml) balsamic vinegar

thick Greek-style yoghurt, to serve

⅓ cup mixed seeds (pumpkin, sunflower, sesame), toasted in a dry frying pan, to serve

1 Preheat oven to 180°C and grease a baking dish.

2 Arrange pumpkin on prepared dish, then sprinkle over cinnamon, mixed spice, salt and pepper. Bake for 20–30 minutes, or until soft.

3 Make dressing by combining olive oil, honey and balsamic vinegar in a jar with a tight-fitting lid, then shaking until it forms an emulsion. About 10 minutes before pumpkin is cooked, remove from oven, sprinkle over dressing, then return to oven for 10 minutes.

4 Serve with a dollop of yoghurt and a sprinkling of seeds.

| NUTRIENT COMPOSITION PER 200 G SERVE: | | | |
|---|---|---|---|
| | Average quantity per serving | %RDI ♀ | ♂ |
| Energy | 1140 kJ (272 kcal) | 13.8 | 11.1 |
| Protein | 6.1 g | 8.5 | 6.8 |
| Carbohydrate | 25.5 g | 11.1 | 8.9 |
| Total fat | 16.5 g | 18.4 | 15.0 |
| Saturated fat | 2.5 g | 17.9 | 9.0 |
| Sodium | 7.5 mg | 0.5 | 0.5 |
| Fibre | 5.3 g | 21.1 | 17.6 |

Pastry-less Spanakopita
with Mixed Greens

# Pearl Barley Risotto with Eggplant, Pumpkin, Sundried Tomatoes, Basil and Feta

## Risotto con orzo perlato, zucca, pomodori secchi e basilico e feta

200 g pumpkin, cut into cubes

¼ cup (60 ml) olive oil

200 g eggplant, cut into cubes

1 medium onion, finely chopped

1 clove garlic, finely chopped

2 cups (400 g) pearl barley, soaked overnight

½ cup (125 ml) white wine

4 cups (1 litre) hot vegetable stock

4 cups (1 litre) hot water

5 sundried tomatoes, sliced

½ cup fresh basil leaves

50 g feta cheese, crumbled

freshly milled sea salt, to taste

freshly ground black pepper, to taste

**Replacing the traditional arborio rice with pearl barley increases the fibre and protein, making this vegetarian dish more filling.**

**1** Preheat oven to 200°C and line a roasting tin with baking paper.

**2** Put pumpkin in prepared roasting tin, drizzle over a third of the olive oil and bake for 30 minutes.

**3** Heat another third of the olive oil in a frying pan over medium heat and lightly fry eggplant. Drain on kitchen paper and set aside.

**4** Heat remaining olive oil in a large saucepan over medium heat, then sauté onion until translucent. Stir through garlic, then add drained pearl barley and wine, and stir for 3–4 minutes, or until wine evaporates.

**5** Add about half a cup of vegetable stock and stir until almost absorbed, then add another half-cup of stock and stir until almost absorbed. Continue adding stock in this way until there's no stock left. Check pearl barley. If not cooked through, slowly add hot water in the same way until barley is cooked.

**6** Stir through sundried tomatoes, pumpkin and eggplant until warmed through, then add basil and top with crumbled feta. Season with salt and pepper, and serve.

**SERVES 4**

### NUTRIENT COMPOSITION PER SERVE:

| | Average quantity per serving | %RDI ♀ | ♂ |
|---|---|---|---|
| Energy | 1465 kJ (350 kcal) | 17.8 | 14.3 |
| Protein | 9.9 g | 13.8 | 11.0 |
| Carbohydrate | 29.1 g | 12.6 | 10.1 |
| Total fat | 20.0 g | 22.3 | 18.3 |
| Saturated fat | 4.6 g | 33.2 | 16.6 |
| Sodium | 1127 mg* | 70.5 | 70.5 |
| Fibre | 7.7 g | 30.9 | 25.7 |

*\* The sodium is high mainly due to the stock. If fresh homemade stock is used, the sodium level will be low.*

# Traditional Flaky Pastry Cheese Pie
## Horiatiki Tiropita

### TRADITIONAL FLAKY PASTRY

3⅓ cups (500 g) bread-making flour,
 plus extra for dusting

1 egg

½ cup (125 ml) lukewarm water

½ teaspoon salt

2 tablespoons olive oil

50 g butter, melted

### FILLING

4 eggs

300 g feta cheese, crumbled

freshly milled sea salt, to taste

freshly ground black pepper, to taste

**NUTRIENT COMPOSITION PER SERVE:**

|  | Average quantity per serving | %RDI ♀ | %RDI ♂ |
|---|---|---|---|
| Energy | 1247 kJ (298 kcal) | 15 | 12 |
| Protein | 11.2 g | 16 | 13 |
| Carbohydrate | 30.5 g | 13 | 11 |
| Total fat | 14.4 g | 16 | 13 |
| Saturated fat | 7.1 g | 51 | 25 |
| Sodium | 426 mg | 27 | 27 |
| Fibre | 1.6 g | 6 | 5 |

Growing up I remember my mother preparing the surface of the kitchen table to make this wonderful buttery and cheesy pie. She had a special rod (I think it was actually a curtain rod made of wood) which she used to roll out the homemade pastry into a large fine sheet. She would sometimes let my sister and I roll out the pastry but we always managed to clump it up onto the rod and she would have to start again. Sometimes she also added sautéed spinach with the feta and egg filling, which was my favourite.

Learning to roll out the pastry was mine and my sister Anna's biggest culinary achievement and now I watch my daughters as they learn to roll out Yiayia's special tiropita pastry.

**1** Preheat oven to 180°C and grease a 30 cm pie dish.

**2** Start by making the pastry. Place the flour in a bowl. Make a well in the centre and stir in egg, lukewarm water and salt. Turn out onto a floured benchtop and knead until soft and smooth. Divide dough into 2 portions.

**3** Combine olive oil and butter in a small bowl. Roll each portion of dough out flat and brush with butter mixture. Fold pastry in half then roll out until at least 40 cm in diameter and fairly thin. Carefully lift the pastry and use it to line prepared pie dish, cutting off any overhanging pastry.

**4** Prepare the filling by beating eggs, stirring in the feta and seasoning with salt and pepper. Pour into pastry case.

**5** Roll out remaining pastry as before, then spread over top of pie, pinching the edges with the bottom layer of pastry to seal. Brush pastry top with remaining butter and oil.

**6** Bake for 40 minutes or until filling is cooked and pie is golden on top. Cut into wedges and serve.

**SERVES 12**

# Soups and Salads

## Salates kai Soupes

# MAKE THE PERFECT SALAD

**Salads are part of every main meal in a traditional Mediterranean diet. Variety in texture and colour is important to boost the fibre content, nutrient value and antioxidant power of the salad. Here's a ten-step guide to preparing the perfect salad.**

Remember the synergies – adding an acid dressing helps the body absorb iron from leafy greens, adding olive oil to the dressing helps the body absorb the carotenoids (lycopene from tomatoes and lutein from leafy greens), and adding herbs doubles the antioxidant uptake from the herbs and salad vegetables.

### Step 1

Choose a variety of leafy greens (go for dark-coloured greens with spicy flavours, such as rocket, kale, dandelion greens, mustard greens, and, if you can find them in specialty markets, amaranth, sow thistle, wild dandelion, wild chicory and purslane). These will ensure you have high concentrations of vitamins A, C, K, calcium and folate, as well as a rich variety of polyphenols. Some of these leafy greens also contain the plant form of omega-3 fats, alpha-linolenic acid (ALA).

### Step 2

Add flavoursome tomatoes – cherry, Roma and heirloom mixed varieties – for their high levels of the antioxidant lycopene.

### Step 3

Add some finely grated root vegetables – carrots, rainbow carrots, beetroot, parsnip, turnip. These add antioxidants called carotenoids and anthocyanins, and are high in fibre and therefore bulky and filling.

### Step 4

Add a mix of seeds and crushed nuts for fibre, iron, calcium, protein (in nuts), polyphenols and healthy monounsaturated and polyunsaturated fats (especially the plant omega-3 ALA).

### Step 5

Add a good-quality extra virgin olive oil for its healthy monounsaturated fats and high levels of polyphenols and other antioxidant and anti-inflammatory substances (hydroxytyrosol, oleuropein and oleocanthal).

### Step 6

Add an acid, such as balsamic vinegar or fresh lemon juice, which can help convert the iron in the leafy greens into a more absorbable form. Acetic acid (in vinegar) is thought to be important for maintaining a healthy gut because it supports friendly bacteria in the intestines.

### Step 7

Add a variety of fresh or dried herbs, which add amazing flavours and are a rich source of antioxidants and anti-inflammatory substances.

### Step 8

To convert a salad to a main meal, add a protein source. For vegetarians this could be a variety of home-cooked or canned legumes or pulses, and for non-vegetarians it could be tuna, salmon, cooked skinless chicken, or grilled lamb, beef or pork fillet (marinated in extra virgin olive oil, herbs, pepper and perhaps even wine).

### Step 9

Dairy lovers could add small quantities of a strong-flavoured cheese (shaved parmesan, crumbled feta) or, for something a little more decadent, creamy blue cheese. Cheese adds valuable calcium and is also a protein source.

### Step 10

Toss everything together to coat the ingredients in the dressing, and enjoy!

# Maria's Sardinian Minestrone
## Minestrone dalla Sardegna

2 tablespoons olive oil

1 large onion, finely chopped

2 medium carrots, chopped

1 celery stalk, leaves reserved, stalk cut into 1 cm pieces

2 cups (500 ml) beef bone stock or vegetable stock

1 × 440 g can diced tomatoes

½ cup Italian soup mix (split pea, bean and lentil mix)

16 cups (4 litres) hot water

¼ butternut pumpkin, cut into cubes

1 large potato, peeled and cut into cubes

200 g green beans, sliced

180 g broccoli florets

180 g cauliflower florets

100 g trimmed cavolo nero or baby spinach leaves

1 tablespoon sea salt

freshly ground black pepper, to taste

1 teaspoon mixed Italian dried herbs or 1 tablespoon chopped fresh basil and thyme

Maria Cincotta is an 80-year-old Italian woman who migrated from the island of the long living people, Sardinia, to Australia in 1960. This recipe was passed on from her grandmother in Italy and Maria still cooks this traditional warm and hearty soup regularly for her family in Australia, especially her grandchildren who love it. This rich vegetable soup is highly nutritious and very low in kilojoules so it's perfect in a weight management plan.

1  Heat olive oil in a large saucepan or stockpot over medium heat and sauté onion, carrot and celery until onion is translucent.

2  Add stock, tomatoes, soup mix and half the water. Bring to a boil, then reduce heat, cover, and simmer for 1 hour.

3  Add pumpkin, potato, green beans, broccoli, cauliflower, cavolo nero (if using baby spinach add just before serving) and remaining hot water. Season with salt and pepper, then cook over low heat for another 1 hour. Stir through baby spinach, if using, and herbs, then serve.

SERVES 10

### NUTRIENT COMPOSITION PER SERVE:

|  | Average quantity per serving | %RDI ♀ | %RDI ♂ |
|---|---|---|---|
| Energy | 448 kJ (107 kcal) | 5 | 4 |
| Protein | 5.3 g | 7 | 6 |
| Carbohydrate | 11.4 g | 5 | 4 |
| Total fat | 4.5 g | 5 | 4 |
| Saturated fat | 0.7 g | 5 | 3 |
| Sodium | 291 mg | 18 | 18 |
| Fibre | 6.0 g | 24 | 20 |

# Vegetable and Lentil Soup
## Soupa fakes me kolokithakia kai karota

2 tablespoons extra virgin olive oil

1 medium red onion, finely chopped

1 clove garlic, finely chopped

6–9 rainbow carrots (orange, purple, yellow), thickly sliced

1 parsnip, cut into small cubes

4 cups (1 litre) water

½ cup (125 ml) puréed tomato

2 ripe tomatoes, chopped

1 cup (185 g) brown lentils

3–4 small yellow baby squash, chopped

1–2 medium zucchini, chopped

freshly milled sea salt, to taste

freshly ground black pepper, to taste

crusty bread, to serve

**This soup is a variation of the traditional Greek lentil soup with colourful root vegetables to boost fibre and antioxidants.**

**1** Heat olive oil in a large saucepan or stockpot over medium heat and sauté onion and garlic until onion is translucent. Add carrots and parsnip, and sauté until they start to soften.

**2** Add water, puréed tomato, fresh tomato and lentils. Bring to a boil, then reduce heat and simmer, covered, for 30 minutes or until lentils are cooked. Some lentil varieties may need more cooking so check and add hot water as required.

**3** Add squash and zucchini, and simmer for a further 15 minutes, or until they are cooked.

**4** Season with salt and pepper, and serve with crusty bread.

**SERVES 6**

### NUTRIENT COMPOSITION PER SERVE:

| | Average quantity per serving | %RDI ♀ | %RDI ♂ |
|---|---|---|---|
| Energy | 953 kJ (228 kcal) | 12 | 9 |
| Protein | 14.3 g | 20 | 16 |
| Carbohydrate | 26.4 g | 12 | 9 |
| Total fat | 7.6 g | 8 | 7 |
| Saturated fat | 1.3 g | 8 | 4 |
| Sodium | 52 mg | 3 | 3 |
| Fibre | 12.0 g* | 48 | 40 |

*\* This dish is very high in fibre.*

# Chick Pea and Spinach Soup
## Soupa me revithia kai spanaki

2 tablespoons extra virgin olive oil

1 medium red onion, finely chopped

1 clove garlic, finely chopped

2 celery stalks, leaves reserved,
   stalks finely sliced

1 medium carrot, thinly sliced

½ teaspoon mixed dried herbs

¼ teaspoon chilli flakes

½ teaspoon salt

½ teaspoon sugar

1 cup (250 ml) puréed tomato

2 × 400 g cans chick peas, drained

4 cups (1 litre) water

1 cup (50 g) baby spinach leaves

You could add grated kefalograviera or parmesan cheese at the end, but note that this will affect the fat and sodium content.

**1** Heat olive oil in a large saucepan over medium heat and sauté onion, garlic, celery and carrot until onion is translucent.

**2** Stir through herbs, chilli flakes, salt, sugar, puréed tomato, chick peas and water. Bring to a boil, then reduce heat and simmer, covered, for about 1 hour.

**3** Just before serving, toss through spinach and season with pepper.

**SERVES 4**

**NUTRIENT COMPOSITION PER SERVE:**

|  | Average quantity per serving | %RDI ♀ | %RDI ♂ |
|---|---|---|---|
| Energy | 1064 kJ (254 kcal) | 13 | 10 |
| Protein | 9.9 g | 14 | 11 |
| Carbohydrate | 25.9 g | 11 | 9 |
| Total fat | 12.4 g | 14 | 11 |
| Saturated fat | 1.8 g | 13 | 6 |
| Sodium | 536 mg | 34 | 34 |
| Fibre | 8.8 g* | 35 | 30 |

*\* This dish is very high in fibre.*

# Mediterranean Salad
## Insalata a la Greco-Italiano

- 1 cup (175 g) burghul, couscous or quinoa
- 1 cup (20 g) fresh mint leaves, chopped
- 1 cup (30 g) chopped fresh flat-leaf parsley
- 2 Lebanese cucumbers, chopped
- 10 Kalamata olives
- 10 Sicilian olives
- 1 cup fresh broad beans, blanched and double-peeled
- 1 cup canned chick peas, drained
- 2–3 tomatoes, chopped
- seeds of 1 pomegranate
- 3–4 spring onions, sliced
- 1 clove garlic or 2 golden shallots, finely sliced
- freshly ground black pepper, to taste

### DRESSING

- 2 tablespoons olive oil
- juice of 1 lemon
- freshly milled sea salt, to taste

My dear friend Rosy Calabro, daughter of Italian migrants from the south of Italy (Calabria), loves to cook and in this salad she has combined classic Italian and Greek ingredients and added a hint of Middle Eastern with the burghul which gives this salad a lovely crunch.

**1** Soak burghul in warm water for 10–15 minutes, then drain and cool. (If using couscous or quinoa, cook according to packet instructions.)

**2** Combine remaining ingredients and sprinkle burghul over the top.

**3** To dress the salad, mix the olive oil with the lemon juice, then drizzle over salad. Season with salt and pepper, toss well and serve.

**SERVES 8**

### NUTRIENT COMPOSITION PER SERVE:

| | Average quantity per serving | %RDI ♀ | ♂ |
|---|---|---|---|
| Energy | 695 kJ (166 kcal) | 8 | 7 |
| Protein | 5.8 g | 8 | 6 |
| Carbohydrate | 17.6 g | 8 | 6 |
| Total fat | 7.9 g | 9 | 7 |
| Saturated fat | 1.2 g | 8 | 4 |
| Sodium | 214 mg | 13 | 13 |
| Fibre | 6.8 g | 27 | 23 |

# Northern Greek Salad
## Horiatiki salata

3–4 Roma tomatoes, sliced

2–3 small Lebanese cucumbers, cut into cubes

1 medium red onion, sliced

½ red capsicum, thinly sliced

½ yellow capsicum, thinly sliced

½ green capsicum, thinly sliced

1 tablespoon capers

2 tablespoons extra virgin olive oil

2 tablespoons red wine vinegar

1 sprig fresh oregano, leaves picked

freshly milled sea salt, to taste

freshly ground black pepper, to taste

80 g feta cheese, crumbled

I grew up with this simple salad which was always at the centre of the table at dinner. The colourful capsicum medley is typical of a Northern Greek dish.

Toss salad vegetables with capers, then dress with olive oil and vinegar. Sprinkle with fresh oregano, season with salt and pepper, toss through feta, and serve.

**SERVES 4**

### NUTRIENT COMPOSITION PER SERVE:

| | Average quantity per serving | %RDI ♀ | %RDI ♂ |
|---|---|---|---|
| Energy | 703 kJ (168 kcal) | 9 | 7 |
| Protein | 5.4 g | 8 | 6 |
| Carbohydrate | 5.1 g | 2 | 2 |
| Total fat | 13.8 g | 15 | 13 |
| Saturated fat | 4.5 g | 32 | 16 |
| Sodium | 257 mg | 17 | 17 |
| Fibre | 2.7 g | 11 | 9 |

# Coral Lettuce with a Spring Onion and Sundried Tomato Vinaigrette

*Marouli me liastes ntomates kai sporia*

1 green and red coral lettuce, washed and roughly chopped

3–4 sundried tomatoes, thinly sliced

4–5 spring onions, thinly sliced

2 tablespoons olive oil

2 tablespoons red wine vinegar or apple cider vinegar

2 tablespoons mixed seeds (pumpkin, sunflower, sesame), toasted in a dry frying pan

freshly milled sea salt, to taste

freshly ground black pepper, to taste

**This delicious salad was inspired during my recent trip to the Greek Islands. Perfect with grilled fresh fish.**

**1** Put lettuce in a large salad bowl.

**2** In a container with a tight-fitting lid, make a dressing by combining sundried tomato, spring onion, olive oil, vinegar and seeds. Season with salt and pepper and shake well.

**3** Pour dressing over lettuce and toss to combine.

**SERVES 4**

### NUTRIENT COMPOSITION PER SERVE:

|  | Average quantity per serving | %RDI ♀ | %RDI ♂ |
|---|---|---|---|
| Energy | 614 kJ (147 kcal) | 8 | 6 |
| Protein | 3.3 g | 5 | 4 |
| Carbohydrate | 4.7 g | 2 | 2 |
| Total fat | 12.7 g | 14 | 12 |
| Saturated fat | 1.9 g | 13 | 7 |
| Sodium | 19 mg | 1 | 1 |
| Fibre | 3.1 g | 13 | 10 |

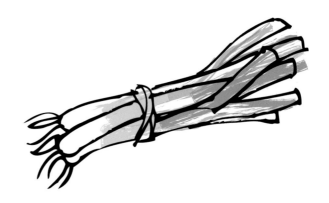

# Rocket Salad with Sundried Tomatoes, Crispy Bacon and Shaved Parmesan

## Salata me roka kai liastes ntomates kai koukounaria

2 tablespoons olive oil

1 tablespoon balsamic vinegar

1 tablespoon honey

freshly milled sea salt, to taste

freshly ground black pepper, to taste

100 g rocket

2 rashers rindless bacon, thinly sliced and fried in a dry non-stick pan until crispy

3–4 sundried tomatoes, thinly sliced

50 g pine nuts, toasted in a dry frying pan

50 g parmesan cheese, shaved

**A perfect light meal when you are spending the day at a beach club on the Greek Islands, or by the pool!**

**1** Make a dressing in a container with a tight-fitting lid by combining oil, vinegar and honey. Season with salt and pepper, then shake well.

**2** Combine rocket with bacon, sundried tomatoes and pine nuts in a salad bowl. Drizzle over dressing and toss well. Top with shaved parmesan and serve.

**SERVES 4**

### NUTRIENT COMPOSITION PER SERVE:

| | Average quantity per serving | %RDI ♀ | %RDI ♂ |
|---|---|---|---|
| Energy | 1306 kJ (312 kcal) | 16 | 13 |
| Protein | 11.4 g | 16 | 13 |
| Carbohydrate | 8.5 g | 4 | 3 |
| Total fat | 26.2 g | 29 | 24 |
| Saturated fat | 5.9 g | 43 | 21 |
| Sodium | 466 mg | 29 | 29 |
| Fibre | 1.7 g | 7 | 6 |

# Spinach, Fig and Anthotiro Salad
## Spanaki me sika kai anthotiro

2 tablespoons tahini

2 tablespoons olive oil

1 tablespoon honey

1 tablespoon white vinegar, or freshly squeezed orange, lemon or lime juice

freshly milled sea salt, to taste

freshly ground black pepper, to taste

2 cups (100 g) baby spinach leaves

4–5 dried figs, soaked in lukewarm water for 30 minutes if too dry, thinly sliced

50 g anthotiro cheese

Anthotiro is a traditional Greek soft whey cheese made with unpasteurised goat's or sheep's milk. Anthotiro literally means 'flower cheese', which refers to the fragrant smell of wild herbs. The cheese no doubt obtains this aroma from goats or sheep that have grazed on such herbs.

1  Make a dressing in a container with a tight-fitting lid by combining tahini, olive oil, honey and vinegar. Season with salt and pepper, then shake well.

2  Combine spinach with figs and anthotiro in a large salad bowl, then drizzle over dressing and toss well.

SERVES 4

NUTRIENT COMPOSITION PER SERVE:

|  | Average quantity per serving | %RDI ♀ | %RDI ♂ |
|---|---|---|---|
| Energy | 1076 kJ (257 kcal) | 13 | 11 |
| Protein | 5.6 g | 8 | 6 |
| Carbohydrate | 19.3 g | 8 | 7 |
| Total fat | 18.0 g | 20 | 16 |
| Saturated fat | 4.0 g | 29 | 14 |
| Sodium | 69 mg | 4 | 4 |
| Fibre | 5.1 g | 20 | 17 |

# Prawn and Black-eyed Bean Salad
## Salata me garides kai mavromatika

16–20 medium whole green prawns

4 cups (1 litre) water

1 bay leaf

½ teaspoon black peppercorns

300 g black-eyed beans

1 tablespoon olive oil

1 medium onion, finely chopped

1 clove garlic, crushed

120 g gourmet lettuce mix

200 g cherry tomatoes, cut in half

½ small hot chilli, deseeded and finely sliced

**DRESSING**

⅓ cup (80 ml) olive oil

juice of 2 lemons

2 tablespoons finely chopped fresh
flat-leaf parsley

freshly milled sea salt, to taste

freshly ground black pepper, to taste

This impressive salad is perfect for a dinner party or long lunch. A highly flavoursome high protein and high fibre meal with relatively low fat content. Perfect with a glass of chilled wine.

1  Peel prawns and retain shells.

2  Wash the shells then pop in a saucepan with water, bay leaf and peppercorns. Bring to a boil, then reduce heat and simmer, covered, for 15 minutes. Drain stock and return to saucepan, setting aside ½ cup (125 ml) for cooking prawns.

3  Add black-eyed beans to stock, return to heat and simmer, covered, for 20–25 minutes, or until beans are soft. Drain and set aside to cool.

4  Heat olive oil in a frying pan over medium heat and sauté onion and garlic until onion is translucent. Add prawns and cook for 3–4 minutes, then add reserved stock to pan, mix through to deglaze pan and set aside to cool.

5  Make the dressing in a container with a tight-fitting lid by combining all ingredients and shaking well.

6  Combine lettuce mix in a salad bowl with tomatoes, chilli, cooled beans and cooked prawns with their cooking juices. Drizzle over dressing and toss well.

**SERVES 6**

**NUTRIENT QUANTITY PER SERVE:**

| | Average quantity per serving | %RDI ♀ | %RDI ♂ |
|---|---|---|---|
| Energy | 1329 kJ (317 kcal) | 16 | 13 |
| Protein | 26.4 g | 37 | 29 |
| Carbohydrate | 22.4 g | 10 | 8 |
| Total fat | 14.1 g | 16 | 13 |
| Saturated fat | 2.3 g | 17 | 8 |
| Sodium | 236 mg | 15 | 15 |
| Fibre | 8.9 g | 35 | 30 |

*Greek Slaw with Red Capsicum Vinaigrette*

# Greek Slaw with Red Capsicum Vinaigrette
## Lahanosalata me karota kai piperies

1 red capsicum

2 tablespoons extra virgin olive oil

2 tablespoons white vinegar

freshly milled sea salt, to taste

freshly ground black pepper, to taste

½ savoy cabbage, finely shredded

1 medium carrot, grated

1–2 tablespoons currants

1 Preheat oven to 180°C.

2 Wrap capsicum in foil and bake for 30–40 minutes, or until very soft. Set aside in foil until cool enough to handle, then deseed capsicum and slice thinly. Retain any juices from the capsicum for the dressing.

3 Make a dressing in a container with a tight-fitting lid by combining the reserved capsicum juices with olive oil and vinegar, seasoning with salt and pepper, and shaking well.

4 Combine cabbage, carrot, currants and capsicum in a salad bowl. Drizzle over dressing and toss well.

SERVES 4

**NUTRIENT COMPOSITION PER SERVE:**

|  | Average quantity per serving | %RDI ♀ | ♂ |
|---|---|---|---|
| Energy | 558 kJ (133 kcal) | 7 | 5 |
| Protein | 3.3 g | 5 | 4 |
| Carbohydrate | 9.1 g | 4 | 3 |
| Total fat | 9.3 g | 10 | 9 |
| Saturated fat | 1.5 g | 10 | 5 |
| Sodium | 46 mg | 3 | 3 |
| Fibre | 5.0 g | 20 | 17 |

# Caprese Salad  Insalata Caprese

5 Roma tomatoes

100 g bocconcini (mini mozzarella) cheese

small bunch (25 g) basil leaves

freshly milled sea salt, to taste

freshly ground black pepper, to taste

1 tablespoon extra virgin olive oil

1 teaspoon balsamic glaze

**This colourful salad which originated in the Campagna region of Italy is thought to have been specifically designed to mirror the Italian flag (red, white and green). This salad can only be made with seasonal vine-ripened tomatoes, fresh soft mozzarella cheese (also called fiore di late) and fresh fragrant basil leaves, and, of course, extra virgin olive oil. Adding balsamic glaze is a modern variant.**

Slice Roma tomatoes into ½ cm thick round slices and arrange on a large salad plate. Slice bocconcini balls into 3–4 slices per ball and arrange a slice on top of each tomato slice. Arrange whole basil leaves on top of each tomato and cheese stack and season with salt and pepper. Drizzle with extra virgin olive oil and a little balsamic glaze over the top of the salad and serve.

**NUTRIENT COMPOSITION PER SERVE:**

|  | Average quantity per serving | %RDI ♀ | ♂ |
|---|---|---|---|
| Energy | 546 kj (130 kcal) | 7 | 5 |
| Protein | 7.3 g | 10 | 8 |
| Carbohydrate | 2.0 g | 1 | 1 |
| Total fat | 10.3 g | 11 | 9 |
| Saturated fat | 4.3 g | 31 | 15 |
| Sodium | 121 mg | 8 | 8 |
| Fibre | 1.0 g | 4 | 3 |

# Baby Cos and Radicchio with Fennel and Pomegranate
## Salata me rantitsio kai rodi

2 baby cos lettuces, leaves separated

½ radicchio, sliced

1 cup (50 g) baby spinach leaves

1 baby fennel, thinly sliced

3–4 radishes, thinly sliced

1–2 Lebanese cucumbers, cut into small cubes

seeds of ½ pomegranate

80–100 g feta cheese, crumbled

### DRESSING

75 ml olive oil

2 tablespoons red wine vinegar

2 teaspoons balsamic vinegar

freshly milled sea salt, to taste

freshly ground black pepper, to taste

I thank my friend Mary Amiridis for this colourful impressive salad combining a mix of sweet and bitter greens garnished with antioxidant-rich pomegranate seeds.

**1** Combine all dressing ingredients in a jar with a tight-fitting lid and shake vigorously.

**2** Combine all salad ingredients in a large bowl, drizzle over dressing and toss well.

**SERVES 6**

**NUTRIENT COMPOSITION PER SERVE:**

| | Average quantity per serving | %RDI ♀ | ♂ |
|---|---|---|---|
| Energy | 804 kJ (192 kcal) | 10 | 8 |
| Protein | 5.0 g | 7 | 6 |
| Carbohydrate | 6.9 g | 3 | 2 |
| Total fat | 15.9 g | 18 | 15 |
| Saturated fat | 4.1 g | 29 | 15 |
| Sodium | 188 mg | 12 | 12 |
| Fibre | 4.9 g | 20 | 16 |

# Spicy Greek Bean Medley
## Fassolakia yiaxni

300 g green beans, trimmed

300 g fresh broad beans, blanched and double-peeled

100 g fresh borlotti beans

100 g freshly podded peas

⅓ cup (80 ml) olive oil

1 medium red onion, finely chopped

1 clove garlic, finely chopped

1 hot red chilli, deseeded (optional) and finely sliced

200 g cherry tomatoes, halved

1–2 bay leaves

⅓ cup (125 ml) water

1 tablespoon fresh dill, finely chopped

freshly milled sea salt, to taste

freshly ground black pepper, to taste

80 g goat's cheese, cut into cubes

few sprigs fresh oregano, leaves picked

**My dear friend Mary Amiridis, inspired by the fresh seasonal beans that are abundant during the summer months, combined a selection of fresh beans with flavoursome tomatoes and a little chilli to bring together this protein and fibre rich salad.**

**1** Steam green, broad and borlotti beans with peas until just cooked.

**2** Meanwhile, heat olive oil in a frying pan over medium heat and sauté onion, garlic and chilli until onion is translucent.

**3** Add in the cherry tomatoes, water, bay leaves and fresh dill and steamed beans and simmer for 10 minutes until beans cooked through.

**4** Season with salt and pepper, pour into serving bowl and garnish with goat's cheese and fresh oregano leaves, and serve.

**SERVES 6**

### NUTRIENT COMPOSITION PER SERVE:

| | Average quantity per serving | %RDI ♀ | ♂ |
|---|---|---|---|
| Energy | 881 kJ (210 kcal) | 11 | 9 |
| Protein | 9.2 g | 13 | 10 |
| Carbohydrate | 7.7 g | 3 | 3 |
| Total fat | 16.0 g | 18 | 15 |
| Saturated fat | 4.0 g | 29 | 14 |
| Sodium | 60 mg | 4 | 4 |
| Fibre | 8.0 g | 32 | 27 |

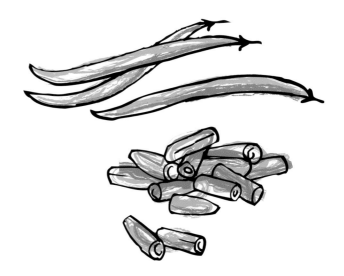

# Greek Frittata
## Omeleta

4 tablespoons olive oil

1 medium potato, peeled and cut into small cubes

1 medium red onion, chopped

1 medium red capsicum, finely chopped

10 olives, pitted and sliced

4 eggs, lightly beaten

30 g feta cheese, crumbled

1 tablespoon chopped fresh flat-leaf parsley, plus extra for garnish

freshly milled sea salt, to taste

freshly ground black pepper, to taste

**This Greek-style omelette can be made with any leftover vegetables you have in the fridge.**

**1** Heat half the olive oil in a frying pan over medium heat and lightly fry the potato pieces, until golden brown and beginning to soften. Remove from pan and drain on kitchen paper.

**2** Add remaining olive oil to frying pan over medium heat and sauté onion until translucent. Add capsicum, olives and potato, then stir-fry lightly for a minute or two.

**3** Add egg, sprinkle over feta and parsley, season with salt and pepper, and cook until the egg sets. Place under grill for 2–3 minutes to set the egg on top, take care not to burn.

**SERVES 2**

### NUTRIENT COMPOSITION PER SERVE:

| | Average quantity per serving | %RDI ♀ | %RDI ♂ |
|---|---|---|---|
| Energy | 1609 kJ (384 kcal) | 22 | 17 |
| Protein | 14.9 g | 24 | 20 |
| Carbohydrate | 13.1 g | 6 | 5 |
| Total fat | 30.4 g | 38 | 31 |
| Saturated fat | 6.1 g | 60 | 30 |
| Sodium | 428 mg | 37 | 37 |
| Fibre | 4.2 g | 17 | 14 |

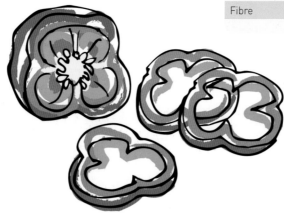

# Rainbow Silverbeet with Rice
## Pilafi me seskoula tri-chromaton

2 tablespoons extra virgin olive oil

1 medium red onion, chopped

1 clove garlic, finely chopped

1 kg rainbow silverbeet/chard, roughly chopped

1 small red chilli, deseeded (optional)
  and finely sliced

1 cup (250 ml) puréed tomato

1 cup (250 ml) water

⅓ cup (80 g) rice

**You can serve this as a vegetarian main dish or as a side dish to a meat-based meal.**

**1** Heat olive oil in a heavy-based medium saucepan over medium heat and sauté onion and garlic until onion is translucent. Add silverbeet and chilli, then sauté for 2–3 minutes, or until silverbeet is wilted.

**2** Add puréed tomato and water, and stir well. Bring to a boil, then reduce heat and simmer, uncovered, for 5 minutes. Add rice and simmer for another 10–15 minutes until rice is cooked.

**3** Remove from heat and allow to stand for 5 minutes before serving.

**SERVES 2 AS A MAIN OR 4 AS A SIDE DISH**

**NUTRIENT COMPOSITION PER MAIN SERVE:**

|  | Average quantity per serving | %RDI ♀ | %RDI ♂ |
|---|---|---|---|
| Energy | 1607 kJ (282 kcal) | 20 | 16 |
| Protein | 8.2 g | 11 | 9 |
| Carbohydrate | 44.7 g | 19 | 16 |
| Total fat | 19.0 g | 21 | 17 |
| Saturated fat | 3.0 g | 21 | 11 |
| Sodium | 433 mg | 27 | 27 |
| Fibre* | 7.6 g | 31 | 25 |

*High in fibre, folate and beta-carotene.*

# Cavolo Nero with Borlotti Beans
## Cavolo nero e fagioli borlotti

2 tablespoons extra virgin olive oil

1 medium red onion, chopped

1 clove garlic, finely chopped

1 bunch (400 g) cavolo nero (Tuscan Kale),
roughly chopped

1 small red chilli, deseeded (optional)
and finely sliced

1 cup (250 ml) puréed tomato

½ cup (125 ml) water

1 × 400 g can borlotti beans, drained

**You can serve this as a vegetarian main dish or as a side dish to a meat-based meal.**

**1**  Heat olive oil in a heavy-based medium saucepan over medium heat and sauté onion and garlic until onion is translucent. Add cavolo nero and chilli, then sauté for 2–3 minutes, or until cavolo nero is wilted.

**2**  Add puréed tomato and water, then stir well. Bring to a boil, then reduce heat and simmer for 5 minutes. Add borlotti beans and simmer for another 5 minutes.

**SERVES 2 AS A MAIN OR 4 AS A SIDE DISH**

### NUTRIENT COMPOSITION PER MAIN SERVE:

| | Average quantity per serving | %RDI ♀ | %RDI ♂ |
|---|---|---|---|
| Energy | 1148 kJ (273 kcal) | 14 | 11 |
| Protein | 9.7 g | 14 | 11 |
| Carbohydrate | 116.1 g | 7 | 6 |
| Total fat | 19.0 g | 21 | 17 |
| Saturated fat | 3.0 g | 21 | 11 |
| Sodium | 170 mg | 11 | 11 |
| Fibre | 11.0 g | 44 | 37 |

*\* Very high in fibre and folate (almost 50 per cent of daily requirements of fibre and folate in one dish).*

# Vegetarian Cabbage Rolls
## Lahanodolmades ladera

⅓ cup (80 ml) extra virgin olive oil,
  plus 40 ml extra

1 medium red onion, finely chopped

1 small red chilli, deseeded (optional)
  and finely sliced

1 medium zucchini, diced

1 medium potato, diced

1 medium carrot, diced

1 medium eggplant, diced

2 tablespoons finely chopped dill

⅓ cup (155 g) pine nuts

1 cup (200 g) rice

1 brown onion, finely diced

1 chopped clove of garlic

1½ cup (375 ml) puréed tomato

1½ cup (375 ml) hot water

1 bay leaf

½ teaspoon chilli flakes

freshly milled sea salt, to taste

freshly ground black pepper, to taste

12 savoy cabbage leaves, blanched for
  3–5 minutes and drained

**1** Preheat oven to 180°C and grease a covered baking dish.

**2** Heat olive oil in a heavy-based saucepan over medium heat and sauté red onion and chilli for 3–4 minutes. Add zucchini, potato, carrot, eggplant, dill, pine nuts and rice, then season to taste and stir well.

**3** Add ½ cup (125 ml) puréed tomato and ½ cup (125 ml) hot water. Bring to a boil, then reduce heat and simmer for 5 minutes. Remove from heat and set aside to cool.

**4** In a separate saucepan, sauté brown onion and garlic in olive oil, add remianing puréed tomato and hot water, bay leaf and chilli flakes, season with salt and pepper, then simmer for 10 minutes then set aside.

**5** Place 2–3 tablespoons of the rice mixture at the bottom of a cabbage leaf. Fold in sides and roll up into a parcel.

**6** Tightly pack the cabbage rolls in the prepared baking dish. Pour tomato liquid into the dish over the rolls. Cover and bake for 45 minutes.

**SERVES 6**

**NUTRIENT COMPOSITION PER SERVE:**

|  | Average quantity per serving | %RDI ♀ | %RDI ♂ |
|---|---|---|---|
| Energy | 1546 kJ (369 kcal) | 19 | 15 |
| Protein | 7.4 g | 10 | 8 |
| Carbohydrate | 39.7 g | 17 | 14 |
| Total fat | 20.1 g | 22 | 18 |
| Saturated fat | 2.5 g | 18 | 9 |
| Sodium | 53 mg | 3 | 3 |
| Fibre | 6.4 g | 26 | 21 |

# Main Dishes

## Kuria Fagita

# Pork and Veal Meatballs in Tomato Sauce
## Polpette

### SAUCE

⅓ cup (80 ml) extra virgin olive oil

1 medium red onion, finely chopped

1 clove garlic, crushed

300 g whole peeled tomatoes

300 ml puréed tomato

1 tablespoon peperonata or finely chopped sundried tomatoes

1 teaspoon dried oregano

pinch of chilli powder

freshly milled sea salt, to taste

freshly ground black pepper, to taste

### MEATBALLS

600 g minced pork and veal

1 onion, finely chopped

1 clove garlic, crushed

2 tablespoons extra virgin olive oil

2 tablespoons breadcrumbs (or rice crumbs for gluten-free)

1 very soft medium tomato, grated (see below)

1 teaspoon dried oregano

pinch of chilli powder

freshly milled sea salt, to taste

freshly ground black pepper, to taste

> **GRATING TOMATOES**
>
> *Cut tomatoes in half. Grate each half with the cut side facing the grater and the skin side in your hand. You should end up with the skin in your hand and no skin in the grated tomato.*

Classic Italian meatballs that feature in spaghetti and meatballs are made with a combination of pork and veal mince.

Serve this as a main dish with a side of polenta, or as sauce for spaghetti.

**1** Start by making the sauce. Heat the oil in a saucepan over medium heat and sauté onion and garlic until onion is translucent. Add tomatoes and puréed tomato, peperonata, oregano, chilli powder, salt and pepper, and stir well. Bring to a boil, then reduce heat and simmer, uncovered, for 30 minutes.

**2** Combine all meatball ingredients and mix well. Roll small pieces of mixture into balls, then sear lightly in a dry non-stick frying pan.

**3** Add meatballs to tomato sauce, then return to a boil and simmer, uncovered, for 1 hour, or until sauce thickens. (Alternatively, bake meatballs in sauce in a preheated oven at 150°C for 1 hour.)

SERVES 6

**NUTRIENT COMPOSITION PER SERVE OF MEATBALLS WITH PASTA:**

|  | Average quantity per serving | %RDI ♀ | %RDI ♂ |
|---|---|---|---|
| Energy | 2716 kJ (649 kcal)* | 33 | 27 |
| Protein | 34.8 g | 48 | 39 |
| Carbohydrate* | 68.9 g | 30 | 24 |
| Total fat | 25.7 g | 29 | 23 |
| Saturated fat | 5.2 g | 37 | 19 |
| Sodium | 160 mg | 10 | 10 |
| Fibre | 6.5 g | 26 | 22 |

*\* When served with salad and no pasta, the kilojoule value is 30 per cent lower (about 1900 kJ) and the carbohydrate value is 10 g per serve.*

# Chicken Meatballs in Saltsa
## Kotokeftedes me saltsa

### SAUCE

⅓ cup (80 ml) extra virgin olive oil

1 medium red onion, finely chopped

1 clove garlic, crushed

2 cups (500 ml) puréed tomato

1 tablespoon peperonata or finely chopped sundried tomatoes

1 bay leaf

1 teaspoon dried oregano

pinch of chilli powder

freshly milled sea salt, to taste

freshly ground black pepper, to taste

### MEATBALLS

500 g minced lean chicken

1 onion, finely chopped

1 clove garlic, crushed

2 tablespoons extra virgin olive oil

2 tablespoons breadcrumbs (or rice crumbs for gluten-free)

1 very soft medium tomato, grated (see page 124)

1 tablespoon finely chopped fresh flat-leaf parsley

1 teaspoon dried oregano

pinch of chilli powder

freshly milled sea salt, to taste

freshly ground black pepper, to taste

**Serve as a main dish on creamy polenta, as sauce for spaghetti, or on potato mash or Cauliflower and Bean Purée (see page 60).**

**1** Start by making the sauce. Heat the oil in a saucepan over medium heat and sauté onion and garlic until onion is translucent. Add puréed tomato, peperonata, bay leaf, oregano, chilli powder, salt and pepper, and stir well. Bring to a boil, then reduce heat and simmer, uncovered, for 30 minutes.

**2** Combine all meatball ingredients and mix well. Roll small pieces of mixture into balls and sear lightly in a dry non-stick frying pan.

**3** Add meatballs to tomato sauce, then return to a boil and simmer, uncovered, for 1 hour, or until sauce thickens. (Alternatively, bake meatballs in sauce in a preheated oven at 150°C for 1 hour.) Remove bay leaf from sauce and serve.

**SERVES 6**

**NUTRIENT COMPOSITION PER SERVE OF MEATBALLS WITH CAULIFLOWER AND BEAN PURÉE:**

|  | Average quantity per serving | %RDI ♀ | ♂ |
|---|---|---|---|
| Energy | 1759 kJ (420 kcal) | 14.6 | 11.8 |
| Protein | 21.0 g | 32.7 | 26.1 |
| Carbohydrate | 13.3 g | 5.3 | 4.3 |
| Total fat | 31.7 g | 18.0 | 14.7 |
| Saturated fat | 6.0 g | 21.2 | 10.6 |
| Sodium | 279 mg | 18.4 | 18.4 |
| Fibre | 6.6 g | 14.0 | 11.7 |

Seafood Balls in Egg
and Lemon Soup
(see page 166)

*Pork and Veal*
*Meatballs in*
*Tomato Sauce*
(see page 124)

*Chicken Meatballs*
*in Saltsa*
(see page 125)

# Tiana and Adam's Paella
## Paella de Valencia

2 tablespoons olive oil, plus extra as required

6 chicken thighs (we chop them but you don't have to)

2 chorizos (about 250 g) (this is a lot because we like it), thinly sliced

1 onion, roughly chopped

1 small capsicum

1⅓ cups (300 g) arborio or medium-grain rice

1 teaspoon paprika

½ teaspoon chilli powder

2–3 saffron fronds, soaked in warm chicken stock (see below)

freshly milled sea salt, to taste

freshly ground black pepper, to taste

1 × 400 g can diced tomatoes

2 cups (500 ml) chicken stock

4 cups (1 litre) water

¾ cup (115 g) peas

This variation of a traditional Spanish paella is a favourite dish of my daughter, Tiana Koutsis, and her friend Adam Spatharis. It is made in a style of Valencian paella (where the dish originated) with chicken and chorizo sausage as the main meat ingredients (rabbit was also used) and a range of vegetables with spices such as saffron and chilli. This recipe is easily scaled up or down and is an easy dish for teenagers and young adults to prepare for the family or their friends (as Tiana and Adam often do).

**1** Heat olive oil in a frying pan over medium heat and lightly sear chicken until slightly golden (it needn't be cooked through completely). Remove chicken from pan and return pan to heat.

**2** Fry chorizo, taking care not to overcook (it fries very quickly!). Remove chorizo from pan and return pan to heat, adding more oil if necessary.

**3** Sauté onion and capsicum until onion is translucent and capsicum limp. Stir in rice, paprika, chilli powder, salt and pepper. Add tomatoes, stock (with saffron) and water, then stir thoroughly. Add chorizo and chicken.

**4** Bring to a boil, then reduce heat and simmer, uncovered, for 20 minutes. Add the peas and continue simmering for another 20 minutes, or until most of the water has been absorbed and the rice is cooked through. If the rice is still hard, add more water and continue cooking until ready.

**SERVES 6**

### NUTRIENT COMPOSITION PER SERVE:

|  | Average quantity per serving | %RDI ♀ | %RDI ♂ |
|---|---|---|---|
| Energy | 2055 kJ (491 kcal) | 25 | 20 |
| Protein | 31.5 g | 44 | 35 |
| Carbohydrate | 46.4 g | 20 | 16 |
| Total fat | 19.8 g | 22 | 18 |
| Saturated fat | 5.7 g | 41 | 21 |
| Sodium | 681 mg | 43 | 43 |
| Fibre | 3.7 g | 15 | 12 |

# Greek Dim Sims
## Lahanodolmades

1 cabbage

2 tablespoons olive oil

1 medium onion, finely chopped

500 g minced lean beef

1 tablespoon finely chopped fresh
  flat-leaf parsley

1 fresh ripe tomato, grated (see page 124)

freshly milled sea salt, to taste

freshly ground black pepper, to taste

4 cups (1 litre) water

½ cup (100 g) rice

2 eggs

juice of 2 lemons

**NUTRIENT COMPOSITION PER SERVE:**

| | Average quantity per serving | %RDI ♀ | %RDI ♂ |
|---|---|---|---|
| Energy | 1254 kJ (300 kcal) | 15 | 12 |
| Protein | 24.2 g | 34 | 27 |
| Carbohydrate | 20.5 g | 9 | 7 |
| Total fat | 13.4 g | 15 | 12 |
| Saturated fat | 3.8 g | 28 | 14 |
| Sodium | 127 mg | 8 | 8 |
| Fibre | 4.9 g | 19 | 16 |

**This dish brings back memories of my childhood where my mother used to roll these lahanodolmades by hand while the cooked cabbage leaves where still boiling hot. The boiled cabbage aroma was not that appealing but I remember the creamy egg and lemon sauce they were cooked in was delicious. This is my husband Savvas' favourite 'mother-in-law's recipe' and he nicknamed the cabbage rolls Greek dim sims!**

**1** Cut stem off bottom of cabbage so that leaves will separate easily and boil whole cabbage in a large saucepan for 30 minutes, or until leaves are cooked through. Take leaves off cabbage and remove from pan as they cook.

**2** Meanwhile, prepare the filling by heating olive oil in a frying pan over medium heat and sautéing onion until translucent. Add mince and cook until lightly browned. Add parsley and tomato, then season with salt and pepper. Add water and bring to a boil, then reduce heat and simmer for 30 minutes.

**3** Stir through rice and continue simmering for about 20 minutes, or until the rice is cooked through. Remove from heat and set aside until cool.

**4** Fill one cabbage leaf at a time, taking care not to tear it. Place leaf on bench top and put 2 tablespoons of the filling at the bottom of the leaf. Fold in sides and roll up into a parcel.

**5** In the same pot that the cabbage was cooking, place a couple of cooked cabbage leaves over the base then arrange the filled cabbage rolls evenly in the bottom of the pot. Continue adding the rolls in layers. Place a plate over the top of cabbage rolls to keep them in place. Pour hot water over plate covering rolls until water level reaches top of plate. Simmer on low heat for 45 minutes.

**6** Remove pot from heat, remove plate and allow to cool slightly.

**7** To prepare sauce, beat eggs lightly and slowly add lemon juice. Take a few spoons of liquid from the cabbage rolls and pour into egg and lemon mix while stirring.

**8** Then slowly pour egg and lemon mixture into pot to form a sauce.

**9** Serve warm with feta cheese and Greek salad.

**SERVES 6 (MAKES ABOUT 20 CABBAGE ROLLS)**

# Pea and Artichoke Casserole with Pork
## Arakas me Hoirino kai Anginares

⅓ cup (80 ml) extra virgin olive oil

1 medium onion, chopped

1 clove garlic, finely chopped

500 g pork fillet, cut into 2 cm dice

½ cup (125 ml) white wine

2 cups (500 ml) puréed tomato

2 cups (500 ml) water

500 g frozen peas

6 fresh artichokes (see below) or 250 g frozen
  artichoke hearts

pinch of cayenne pepper

freshly milled sea salt, to taste

freshly ground black pepper, to taste

**Serve this hearty casserole with steamed rice, mashed potato or a salad.**

**1** Heat olive oil in a large saucepan over medium heat and sauté onion and garlic until onion is translucent. Add pork and brown lightly on all sides. Add wine and simmer until mostly evaporated. Stir through puréed tomato and water. Bring to a boil, then reduce heat and simmer, uncovered, for 20 minutes.

**2** Add peas and simmer for another 10 minutes. Add artichokes and simmer for another 10 minutes. The casserole should be moist but not too soupy. Cook for longer if necessary, but take care not to overcook the meat.

**3** Stir through cayenne pepper, season with salt and pepper, and serve.

SERVES 6

### PREPARING ARTICHOKES

* *Fill a bowl with cold water and add the juice of 1 lemon.*
* *Cut off most of the large stalk at the base of the flower, leaving enough to hold onto.*
* *Keep removing the outer leaves until you reach the soft ones and expose the heart.*
* *Using a sharp knife, remove and discard the choke.*
* *Trim off the remaining stem.*
* *Rub each prepared artichoke heart with a lemon half, then drop into the lemon water to prevent browning.*

### NUTRIENT COMPOSITION PER SERVE:

|  | Average quantity per serving | %RDI ♀ | %RDI ♂ |
|---|---|---|---|
| Energy | 1277 kJ (305 kcal) | 16 | 13 |
| Protein | 28.8 g | 40 | 32 |
| Carbohydrate | 13.1 g | 6 | 5 |
| Total fat | 14.2 g | 16 | 13 |
| Saturated fat | 2.4 g | 17 | 9 |
| Sodium | 123 mg | 8 | 8 |
| Fibre* | 18.9 g | 76 | 63 |

* *Combine this meal with a salad and you would meet your daily fibre needs in one sitting.*

# Chicken, Cherry Tomato and Spinach Risoni *Giouvetsi me kotopoulo*

2¼ cups (500 g) risoni pasta

¼ cup (60 ml) olive oil

500 g chicken thigh fillets, cut into cubes

40 g Greek loukaniko or chorizo, sliced

½ cup (125 ml) white wine

1 clove garlic, finely chopped

200 g cherry tomatoes, cut in half

¾ cup (190 ml) puréed tomato

1 cup (250 ml) water

½ small chilli, deseeded and finely sliced

1 cup (50 g) baby spinach leaves

75 g feta cheese, crumbled

1 tablespoon chopped fresh flat-leaf parsley

freshly milled sea salt, to taste

freshly ground black pepper, to taste

**A quick paella-style dish that can be prepared in less than 30 minutes.**

**1** Parboil risoni in boiling water for 5 minutes, then drain, reserving ½ cup (125 ml) of the cooking water.

**2** Meanwhile, in another saucepan, heat olive oil over medium heat and sauté chicken until browned. Add loukaniko and sauté for a few more minutes. Add wine and simmer until it evaporates. Remove chicken and loukaniko from pan and set aside.

**3** Add garlic and sauté for a minute or so, then add cherry tomatoes, puréed tomato, water and chilli. Stir well and bring to a boil, then reduce heat and simmer, uncovered, for 10 minutes.

**4** Return chicken and loukaniko to pan with parboiled risoni and reserved cooking water and simmer until risoni is cooked. Add spinach and stir through gently until wilted. Add feta and parsley, season with salt and pepper, and serve.

**SERVES 6**

### NUTRIENT COMPOSITION PER SERVE:

| | Average quantity per serving | %RDI ♀ | ♂ |
|---|---|---|---|
| Energy | 2431 kJ (581 kcal) | 44 | 36 |
| Protein | 30.8 g | 64 | 51 |
| Carbohydrate | 61.9 g | 40 | 32 |
| Total fat | 21.9 g | 37 | 30 |
| Saturated fat | 7.0 g | 75 | 37 |
| Sodium | 417 mg | 39 | 39 |
| Fibre | 4.4 g | 27 | 22 |

# Slow-cooked Beef Cheek and Eggplant Casserole
## Magoulo vodino me melintzanes yiaxni

½ cup (125 ml) olive oil

1 onion, finely chopped

2 cloves garlic, finely chopped

1 kg beef cheeks

1 cup (250 ml) white wine

1 cup (250 ml) puréed tomato

2 bay leaves

1 sprig fresh rosemary

½ teaspoon ground cinnamon

1 teaspoon black peppercorns

4 cups (1 litre) water

2 large eggplants

salt

freshly milled sea salt, to taste

freshly ground black pepper, to taste

**Serve on mashed potato or rice, or with a green salad as a low-carb option.**

**1** Preheat oven to 160°C.

**2** Heat half the olive oil in a heavy-based flameproof casserole dish on the stovetop and sauté onion and garlic until onion is translucent. Add beef and brown lightly on all sides. Add wine and simmer until mostly evaporated. Add puréed tomato, herbs, spices and water, then stir well. Bring to a boil, then reduce heat and simmer, uncovered, for 10 minutes.

**3** Put the lid on the casserole dish and bake for 2 hours. (Alternatively, cook for 1 hour in a pressure cooker on the stovetop.)

**4** Meanwhile, cut eggplant into large cubes, sprinkle all over with salt and leave in a colander for 20 minutes. Rinse under cold running water and dry on kitchen paper.

**5** Heat remaining olive oil in a frying pan over medium heat and fry eggplant until lightly browned. Drain on kitchen paper.

**6** When beef has been cooking for 2 hours, remove from oven and add eggplant with another 1–2 cups (250–500 ml) water (as required). Season with salt and pepper then return to oven and bake for another 30 minutes.

**7** When serving, pull beef cheeks apart into 6–8 portions.

**SERVES 8**

### NUTRIENT COMPOSITION PER SERVE:

| | Average quantity per serving | %RDI ♀ | %RDI ♂ |
|---|---|---|---|
| Energy | 1437 kJ (343 kcal) | 17 | 14 |
| Protein | 28.5 g | 40 | 32 |
| Carbohydrate | 4.5 g | 2 | 2 |
| Total fat | 22.1 g | 25 | 20 |
| Saturated fat | 5.3 g | 38 | 19 |
| Sodium | 102 mg | 6 | 6 |
| Fibre | 2.6 g | 11 | 9 |

# Slow-cooked Beef Casserole
## Tas Kebab

½ cup (125 ml) extra virgin olive oil

2 onions, finely chopped

2 cloves garlic, finely chopped

1 kg rump steak

1 cup (250 ml) puréed tomato

2 bay leaves

1 tablespoon sweet paprika

1 teaspoon black peppercorns

4 cups (1 litre) water

freshly milled sea salt, to taste

### NUTRIENT COMPOSITION PER SERVE:

| | Average quantity per serving | %RDI ♀ | ♂ |
|---|---|---|---|
| Energy | 1255 kJ (300 kcal) | 15 | 12 |
| Protein | 26.4 g | 37 | 29 |
| Carbohydrate | 3.7 g | 2 | 1 |
| Total fat | 20.1 g | 22 | 18 |
| Saturated fat | 4.4 g | 32 | 16 |
| Sodium | 89 mg | 6 | 6 |
| Fibre | 1.6 g | 7 | 5 |

Tas Kebab is popular in the Greek cuisine but not traditionally Greek, having originated from Asia Minor Greeks who resettled in the mainland. We loved ths home-cooked dish as I was growing up. When my sister tried to document recipes from our mum, a very proud cook, she said 'εγω δεν μετραω, Οσο παρι και θα το δοκιμασεις'. Translation: I do not measure ingredients when I cook, you add as much as it needs and you keeping tasting it until it is right. My sister Anna managed to capture this family favourite.

1 Heat olive oil in a large heavy-based pot or saucepan over medium heat on the stovetop. Sauté onion and garlic until onion is translucent. Add beef and brown lightly on all sides. Add puréed tomato, bay leaves, paprika, peppercorns and water. Bring to a boil, then reduce heat and simmer, covered, over low heat for 2 hours. (Alternatively, you can use a pressure cooker and cut the cooking time down to 1 hour.)

2 Season with salt, if necessary, and serve with rice or Cauliflower and Bean Purée (see page 60).

SERVES 8

# Beef Stifado
## Stifado vodino

¼ cup (60 ml) olive oil

1 red onion, finely chopped

2 cloves garlic, finely chopped

600 g rump steak, cut into large cubes

½ cup (125 ml) red wine

1 large ripe tomato, cut into cubes

2 tablespoons tomato paste

½ teaspoon ground nutmeg

1 teaspoon black peppercorns

1 teaspoon whole cloves

2 bay leaves

8 cups (2 litres) hot water

1 kg golden shallots, peeled and left whole

1½ tablespoons brandy (we use Metaxa 5 Star)

2 tablespoons balsamic vinegar

freshly milled sea salt, to taste

freshly ground black pepper, to taste

50g toasted pine nuts

handful of chopped parsley, for garnish

The cooking time for this dish depends on the cut of meat you use. It also works well with shoulder or chuck steak, but these will need to be cooked for an extra hour.

1 Heat half the olive oil in large, heavy-based saucepan over medium heat and sauté red onion and garlic until onion is translucent. Add rump steak and brown lightly on all sides. Add wine and simmer until mostly evaporated. Add fresh tomato, tomato paste, nutmeg, peppercorns, cloves, bay leaves and half the hot water. Bring to a boil, then reduce heat and simmer, covered, for 1 hour.

2 In a separate frying pan, lightly sauté golden shallots in the remainder of the olive oil until they start to become translucent, add brandy and vinegar and stir until alcohol is evaporated. Transfer shallots to meat casserole, add remaining hot water, and cook on low heat for another 1 hour. Season with salt and pepper.

3 Serve with rice, polenta or potato mash and greens such as broccolini. To make broccolini, steam for 5 minutes, transfer to dish and dress with extra virgin olive oil, fresh lemon juice, ½ clove garlic (minced) and season with salt and pepper. Garnish with parsley and toasted pine nuts.

SERVES 6

**COOK IN HALF THE TIME IN PRESSURE COOKER:**
*Once meat is browned, add spices, 3 cups (750 ml) hot water and cook for 30 minutes. Remove from heat, open lid and add sautéed onions, then cover and cook for another 15 minutes.*

### NUTRIENT COMPOSITION PER SERVE:

| | Average quantity per serving | %RDI ♀ | %RDI ♂ |
|---|---|---|---|
| Energy | 1213 kJ (290 kcal) | 15 | 12 |
| Protein | 24.2 g | 34 | 27 |
| Carbohydrate | 10.6 g | 5 | 4 |
| Total fat | 14.5 g | 16 | 13 |
| Saturated fat | 3.2 g | 23 | 12 |
| Sodium | 79 mg | 5 | 5 |
| Fibre | 5.4 g | 22 | 18 |

# Roast Pork Fillet
## Hoirino fileto sto fourno

600 g pork fillet

⅓ cup (80 ml) extra virgin olive oil

½ cup (125 ml) water

a few sprigs fresh rosemary, leaves picked

juice of 1 lemon

freshly milled sea salt, to taste

freshly ground black pepper to taste

**NUTRIENT COMPOSITION PER SERVE
WITH SLOW-BAKED ROOT VEGETABLES:**

| | Average quantity per serving | %RDI ♀ | %RDI ♂ |
|---|---|---|---|
| Energy | 1567 kJ (374 kcal) | 19 | 15 |
| Protein | 25.6 g | 36 | 28 |
| Carbohydrate | 20.1 g | 9 | 7 |
| Total fat | 21.3 g | 24 | 19 |
| Saturated fat | 3.6 g | 26 | 13 |
| Sodium | 106 mg | 7 | 7 |
| Fibre | 5.6 g | 22 | 19 |

**A dish that can be prepared within half an hour after work. Pork fillet is so tender that it only needs 20 minutes in the oven.**

**1** Preheat oven to 180°C.

**2** Rub pork fillets all over with olive oil and place in a heavy-based flameproof casserole dish over medium heat on the stovetop. Lightly seal the pork on each side. Pour in water and sprinkle in rosemary.

**3** Bake for about 15 minutes, or until pork is cooked through.

**4** Transfer pork to a carving plate to rest for 5 minutes, then cut into thick slices.

**5** Return casserole dish to stovetop and add lemon juice. Stir to deglaze pan, then pour juices over meat. Season with salt and pepper.

**6** Serve with steamed broccolini (see page 140) or Slow-baked Root Vegetables (see page 75).

**SERVES 6**

# Open Lamb Souvlaki with Spicy Tzatziki
## Arnisio souvlaki me pita

1 teaspoon dried oregano or mixed herbs

freshly milled sea salt, to taste

freshly ground black pepper, to taste

500 g lamb backstrap

olive oil, for greasing

grilled pita bread, to serve

salad, to serve

tomato cut into wedges, to serve

### SPICY TZATZIKI

1 small Lebanese cucumber, peeled

1 clove garlic, finely chopped

1–2 tablespoons dill, finely chopped

1 cup (260 g) thick Greek-style yoghurt

1 tablespoon olive oil

1 tablespoon white vinegar

¼–½ teaspoon cayenne pepper

freshly milled sea salt, to taste

freshly ground black pepper, to taste

This is a perfect quick family meal where everyone participates by rolling their own souvlaki. It can easily be scaled up for large group functions.

1 Sprinkle herbs and salt and pepper over lamb, turning to coat all over, place in dish and cover and set aside to marinate for 30 minutes in the refrigerator.

2 Meanwhile, prepare the tzatziki. Grate cucumber and squeeze out extra juice, then toss in a bowl with garlic and dill. Stir through yoghurt, then add olive oil, vinegar and cayenne pepper, and season with salt and pepper. Refrigerate until ready to use.

3 Preheat a barbecue or chargrill pan. Grease with a little olive oil and grill lamb for 10–15 minutes, or to your liking, turning halfway during cooking time.

4 Serve with tzatziki, pita bread, salad and tomato wedges.

SERVES 4

### NUTRIENT COMPOSITION PER SERVE WITH PITA BREAD AND SALAD:

|  | Average quantity per serving | %RDI ♀ | %RDI ♂ |
|---|---|---|---|
| Energy | 1679 kJ (401 kcal) | 21 | 16 |
| Protein | 35.9 g | 50 | 40 |
| Carbohydrate | 39.8 g | 17 | 14 |
| Total fat | 10.6 g | 12 | 10 |
| Saturated fat | 4.0 g | 29 | 14 |
| Sodium | 535 mg | 33 | 33 |
| Fibre | 4.4 g | 18 | 15 |

**NUTRIENT COMPOSITION PER SERVE:**

|  | Average quantity per serving | %RDI ♀ | ♂ |
|---|---|---|---|
| Energy | 1257 kJ (300 kcal) | 15 | 12 |
| Protein | 36.0 g | 50 | 40 |
| Carbohydrate | 7.0 g | 3 | 2 |
| Total fat | 14.1 g | 16 | 13 |
| Saturated fat | 2.5 g | 18 | 9 |
| Sodium | 257 mg | 16 | 16 |
| Fibre | 5.3 g | 21 | 18 |

# Grilled Chicken Skewers on Sicilian Caponata
## Caponata siciliana con pollo alla griglia

1 teaspoon mixed dried herbs

½ teaspoon paprika

freshly milled sea salt, to taste

freshly ground black pepper, to taste

600 g chicken tenderloins

8 souvlaki skewers (soaked in water for 30 minutes to prevent burning)

**CAPONATA**

1 medium eggplant

salt

¼ cup (60 ml) extra virgin olive oil

1 large red onion, roughly chopped

1 clove garlic, finely chopped

2 celery stalks, finely chopped

½ small yellow capsicum, finely chopped

½ small red capsicum, finely chopped

½ small green capsicum, finely chopped

200 g cherry tomatoes, cut in half

½ cup (125 ml) puréed tomato

10 green Sicilian olives, pitted and sliced

10 black olives, pitted and sliced

1 tablespoon capers

2 tablespoons red wine vinegar

1 tablespoon caster sugar

2 tablespoons chopped fresh basil

freshly ground black pepper, to taste

Caponata is a traditional Italian vegetarian dish from Sicily is based on eggplant and many other vegetables cut into small cubes and sautéed in extra virgin olive oil and a sweet and sour sauce. Caponata implies 'sweet and sour' in Italian, others believe it originated in Spain and means 'tied together like vines'. Whatever the origin it makes a great tasting side dish and is low in kilojoules due to the low carbohydrate vegetables.

**1** Mix herbs, paprika, salt and pepper in a large bowl, and add chicken, making sure the tenderloins are covered all over. Cover and refrigerate for 1 hour.

**2** Meanwhile, prepare the caponata. Cut eggplant into small cubes, sprinkle all over with salt and leave in a colander for 20 minutes. Rinse under cold running water and dry on kitchen paper.

**3** Heat half the olive oil in a frying pan over medium heat and fry eggplant until lightly browned. Drain on kitchen paper.

**4** Heat remaining olive oil in frying pan over medium heat and sauté onion, garlic and celery until onion is translucent. Add all three capsicums and sauté until they start to soften. Add eggplant, cherry tomatoes, puréed tomato, olives and capers, and cook briefly.

**5** When just simmering, stir through vinegar and sugar. Bring to a boil, reduce heat and simmer, uncovered, for 20–25 minutes, or until vegetables are soft and sauce is thick and shiny.

**6** While caponata is cooking, thread marinated chicken onto souvlaki skewers and preheat a barbecue or chargrill pan. Cook the skewers, turning to ensure even cooking.

**7** Stir basil through caponata, season with pepper, and serve with chicken skewers.

SERVES 4

# Sav's Gyros

250 g ripe tomatoes, roughly chopped

250 g red capsicums, roughly chopped

125 g red onions, roughly chopped

½ cup (125 ml) white wine

1 kg lamb shoulder, cut into palm-sized slices (ask your butcher to do this)

1 kg chicken thigh fillets

2 teaspoons sea salt

1 teaspoon black pepper

3 teaspoons oregano

### NUTRIENT COMPOSITION PER SERVE:

| | Average quantity per serving | %RDI ♀ | %RDI ♂ |
|---|---|---|---|
| Energy | 1178 kJ (281 kcal) | 14 | 12 |
| Protein | 39.6 g | 55 | 44 |
| Carbohydrate | 2.2 g | 1 | 1 |
| Total fat | 12.1 g | 13 | 11 |
| Saturated fat | 4.2 g | 30 | 15 |
| Sodium | 608 mg | 38 | 38 |
| Fibre | 1.1 g | 4 | 4 |

This is a traditional lamb dish cooked on a rotisserie over a charcoal fire. It is called gyros (which literally means turning around) because the meat cooks as it rotates around a rotisserie.

The gyros meat tastes best if allowed to marinate overnight, but if you don't have that much time, a couple of hours will do it. My husband Savvas would always prepare this (at least 8–10 kg of meat) for parties and spend hours puréeing the marinade with his mother, Paraskevi.

1  Whizz tomato, capsicum and onion in a food processor until they form a pulp, then stir through wine.

2  Take 2 large bowls, one for the lamb and one for the chicken. In each bowl, put a layer of meat on the bottom, season with salt, pepper and oregano, add a little tomato sauce and keep layering until all the meat is in the bowls. Pour over any remaining marinade. Cover bowls and marinate in the refrigerator for at least 2 hours but preferably overnight.

3  Preheat a barbecue or chargrill pan. Take large skewer (such as a rotisserie rod) and thread the lamb pieces on one end and the chicken pieces on the other (or alternate lamb and chicken if you prefer).

4  Grill the meat until cooked through (Greeks prefer well done, with a good amount of charcoal). Using a sharp knife or electric knife, slowly shave off cooked meat from the outer edge of the gyros, squeeze fresh lemon juice over meat and serve with spicy tzatziki and Greek salad.

5  The recipe can be scaled up for large groups. This recipe x 4 with 3–4 salads can feed a group of 16 people.

**SERVES 4**

# Slow-roasted Goat
## Katsiki sto fourno

2–3 kg goat (shoulder with ribs or leg, yielding about 1.5–1.8 kg meat)

⅓ cup (80 ml) olive oil

freshly milled sea salt, to taste

freshly ground black pepper, to taste

2–3 sprigs fresh rosemary, leaves picked

1 cup (250 ml) water

8 whole baby potatoes, unpeeled

6–9 rainbow carrots (orange, purple, yellow)

10 baby beetroot, topped and peeled

Greek Slaw with Red Pepper Vinaigrette (see page 109), to serve

**A variation on the traditional Greek slow-roasted lamb dish, goat is preferred on the mountainous islands of Greece such as Crete.**

**1** Preheat oven to 150°C.

**2** Rub goat all over with half the olive oil and season well with salt and pepper.

**3** Sit goat on a large piece of aluminium foil, sprinkle with fresh rosemary, then wrap and sit in a roasting tin. Pour in half the water and slow-bake for 90 minutes. Remove goat from oven and carefully unwrap from foil.

**4** Line the base of the same roasting tin with potatoes, carrots and beetroot. Season well with salt and pepper and the remaining olive oil and sit goat in the centre. Add remaining water and return to oven for another 90 minutes.

**5** When the goat is cooked, it should pull apart easily. Serve goat and roasted vegetables with Greek Slaw.

**SERVES 8–10**

### NUTRIENT COMPOSITION PER 260 G SERVE OF MEAT

| | Average quantity per serving | %RDI ♀ | %RDI ♂ |
|---|---|---|---|
| Energy | 1527 kJ (363 kcal) | 18 | 15 |
| Protein | 39.5 g | 54 | 44 |
| Carbohydrate | 12.3 g | 5 | 4 |
| Total fat | 17.4 g | 20 | 16 |
| Saturated fat | 5.4 g | 39 | 19 |
| Sodium | 112 mg | 7 | 7 |
| Fibre | 3.7 g | 15 | 13 |

# Greek Dish with a Twist – Deconstructed Moussaka

6 large red capsicums

2 tablespoons extra virgin olive oil

1 large potato, peeled and cut into small cubes

1 eggplant, cut into small cubes

½ cup (125 ml) water

### MINCE FILLING

¼ cup (60 ml) extra virgin olive oil, plus extra for drizzling

1 red onion, finely chopped

1 clove garlic, crushed

500 g minced lean beef

½ cup (125 ml) white wine

1 cup (250 ml) puréed tomato

chilli powder, to taste

1 teaspoon mixed dried herbs

8 cups (2 litres) hot water

1 tablespoon finely chopped fresh flat-leaf parsley

freshly milled sea salt, to taste

freshly ground black pepper, to taste

### BÉCHAMEL

50 g butter

½ cup (75 g) plain (or gluten-free) flour

2 cups (500 ml) milk

salt, to taste

SERVES 6

I was inspired to modify this dish when I recently visited the Island of Zakinthos in Greece. Here is my version with red capsicum stuffed with a moussaka–style mince and diced potato and eggplant.

**1** Using a sharp knife, cut across the top of each capsicum to make a lid, leaving it attached on one side. (Don't worry if you cut the lid off completely – you can still sit it on top). Scoop out the seeds with a small spoon.

**2** Heat olive oil in a frying pan over medium heat and lightly fry potato and eggplant, then remove from pan and drain on kitchen paper.

**3** To make mince filling, heat olive oil in frying pan over medium heat and sauté onion and garlic until onion is translucent. Add mince, breaking it up as you go, and cook until lightly browned. Add wine and cook until it evaporates. Add puréed tomato, chilli powder, herbs and half the water. Bring to a boil, then reduce heat and simmer, uncovered, for 1 hour. As water evaporates, add remaining water to prevent mince from drying out.

**4** Stir through potato, eggplant and parsley, season with salt and pepper, then remove from heat and set aside to cool slightly.

**5** Preheat oven to 180°C. Arrange capsicums in a roasting tin side by side so they retain their shape and stay upright during cooking. Flip lids to one side and fill each capsicum almost to the top with mince filling. Set aside.

**6** To make the béchamel, heat butter in a heavy-based, non-stick saucepan over medium heat until it starts to froth. Stir in flour and cook until mixture starts to brown lightly and swell. Gradually add milk, stirring well to combine, then continue stirring until sauce thickens. (If lumps form, break them up with a whisk.) Season with salt.

**7** Lift each capsicum lid and spoon a dollop of béchamel on top of mince filling, leaving capsicum lids to the side. Drizzle a little olive oil over capsicums and pour ½ cup (125 ml) water into tin. Bake for 45 minutes, or until béchamel is lightly browned on top.

**8** Allow to cool for 10 minutes before serving. Flip lids on top of béchamel and serve.

| NUTRIENT COMPOSITION PER SERVE: | | | |
|---|---|---|---|
| | Average quantity per serving | %RDI | |
| | | ♀ | ♂ |
| Energy | 2047 kJ (489 kcal) | 25 | 20 |
| Protein | 25.3 g | 35 | 28 |
| Carbohydrate | 26.3 g | 11 | 9 |
| Total fat | 30.7 g | 34 | 28 |
| Saturated fat | 10.9 g | 78 | 40 |
| Sodium | 189 mg | 12 | 12 |
| Fibre | 5.1 g | 21 | 17 |

# Chicken Saganaki
## Kotopoulo fileto saganaki

2 tablespoons extra virgin olive oil

1 red onion, finely chopped

2 cloves garlic, crushed

600 g chicken tenderloins (or thigh fillets)

1 × 400 g can whole peeled Roma tomatoes

1 cup (250 ml) water

1 small chilli, deseeded (optional) and finely
sliced, or ½ teaspoon chilli flakes

2 tablespoons pitted and sliced Kalamata olives

1 teaspoon dried mixed herbs

80 g feta cheese, crumbled

2 tablespoons finely chopped fresh
flat-leaf parsley

Saganaki in Greek means small frying pan. It is also a style of cooking, such as for frying appetisers (mezedes). In Greek restaurants saganaki is commonly fried kefalograviera cheese (sometimes lightly floured before frying). Prawn saganaki is also commonly served (see page 162).

My sister, Anna, often whips up this family favourite as a quick after-work meal.

1  Heat olive oil in a frying pan over medium heat and sauté onion until translucent. Add garlic and chicken fillets and lightly brown chicken on all sides. Add tomatoes, water, chilli, olives and herbs. Bring to a boil, then reduce heat and simmer, uncovered, for 15 minutes.

2  Sprinkle over feta and parsley, then serve with rice or a Greek salad.

SERVES 4

NUTRIENT COMPOSITION PER SERVE:

|  | Average quantity per serving | %RDI ♀ | %RDI ♂ |
|---|---|---|---|
| Energy | 1475 kJ (352 kcal) | 18 | 14 |
| Protein | 38.8 g | 54 | 43 |
| Carbohydrate | 5.2 g | 2 | 2 |
| Total fat | 19.4 g | 22 | 18 |
| Saturated fat | 5.6 g | 40 | 20 |
| Sodium | 579 mg | 36 | 36 |
| Fibre | 3.5 g | 14 | 12 |

# Vasiliki Patsakos's Chicken Pie
## Kotopita

1 small chicken

1 quantity Traditional Flaky Pastry (see page 84) or purchased puff pastry

¼ cup (60 ml) olive oil, plus extra for pastry

1 medium onion, finely chopped

1½ cups (300 g) rice

½ cup finely chopped fresh flat-leaf parsley

2 tablespoons finely chopped fresh dill

5 spring onions, thinly sliced

freshly milled sea salt, to taste

freshly ground black pepper, to taste

### NUTRIENT COMPOSITION PER SERVE:

| | Average quantity per serving | %RDI ♀ | ♂ |
|---|---|---|---|
| Energy | 1745 kJ (417 kcal) | 21 | 17 |
| Protein | 30.3 g | 42 | 34 |
| Carbohydrate | 42.0 g | 18 | 15 |
| Total fat | 13.9 g | 16 | 13 |
| Saturated fat | 2.9 g | 20 | 10 |
| Sodium | 456 mg | 29 | 29 |
| Fibre | 1.5 g | 6 | 5 |

### QUICK VERSION:

* *Use puff pastry but you only need one layer each for the bottom and top.*
* *Use roast chicken, remove meat and shred (discard skin).*
* *Replace chicken stock with ready-made chicken stock (liquid stock).*

This traditional Northern Greek chicken pie has been a favourite family meal of my friend, Helen Karikas, who has inherited this recipe from her mother, Vasiliki Patsakos. I spent a day with Helen and her mum, who has just turned 80, and learnt how to make this favourite dish.

**1** Preheat oven to 200°C and grease a 30 cm pie dish.

**2** Put chicken in a stockpot with enough water to cover and bring to a boil over medium heat. Reduce heat and simmer, covered, for 90 minutes, or until meat is falling off the bone. Drain, retaining 5 cups (1.25 litres) of the stock, and set chicken aside, covered, until cool enough to handle, then remove meat from bones and shred it into a bowl. Set aside.

**3** Divide pastry into 5 portions and roll 3 of those portions out thinly to 30 cm diameter. Put the first portion in the base of the prepared dish. Sprinkle with a little olive oil then add the second portion on top. Sprinkle with olive oil again, then add the third portion.

**4** Heat olive oil in a frying pan over medium heat and sauté onion until translucent. Add rice and cook, stirring frequently, until rice starts to become translucent. Add fresh herbs and spring onions, and cook until wilted.

**5** Slowly add 4 cups (1 litre) of the reserved chicken stock. Bring to a boil, then reduce heat and simmer, uncovered, for 20 minutes, or until rice is almost cooked. Add shredded chicken and stir well.

**6** Pour rice and chicken filling on top of pastry in pie dish. Roll out the remaining 2 portions of pastry to 30 cm. Place one on top of filling, then brush with olive oil and add the second. Cut a few slits on top of pie, brush with olive oil, and bake for 30 minutes, or until golden on top.

**7** Remove from oven, pour remaining reserved stock over pie, then return to oven for 5 minutes to crisp up pastry.

SERVES 8

# Fish and Seafood

## Thalassina

# White Anchovies
## Gavros

500 g fresh sardines (or pilchards)

1 cup (250 ml) red or white wine vinegar

2 cloves garlic, finely chopped

chopped fresh or dried herbs, to taste

finely chopped fresh chillies or chilli powder,
  to taste

¼ cup (60 ml) extra virgin olive oil,
  plus extra for drizzling

crusty bread, to serve

chopped tomato, to serve

chopped red onion, to serve

chopped fresh red chilli, for garnish

### NUTRIENT COMPOSITION PER 50 G SERVE:

| | Average quantity per serving | %RDI | |
| --- | --- | --- | --- |
| | | ♀ | ♂ |
| Energy | 477 kJ (114 kcal) | 6 | 5 |
| Protein | 10.3 g | 14 | 11 |
| Carbohydrate | 0.3 g | 0 | 0 |
| Total fat | 7.6 g | 8 | 7 |
| Saturated fat | 1.4 g | 10 | 5 |
| Sodium | 38 mg | 2 | 2 |
| Fibre | 0.6 g | 2 | 2 |

Fresh they are sardines but when pickled they are called anchovies. The best way to enjoy white anchovies is with crusty bread, slices of cucumber, a few olives and a serve of ouzo with ice while sailing the Ionian Sea. Alternatively, serve as a mezze to a gathering of friends on a lovely summer afternoon with a shot of ouzo on ice and dream of the Mediterranean.

1 Scale sardines and remove intestines, head and tail. Wash thoroughly. (You can fillet the sardines at this stage if you're comfortable doing this.) Open them out, butterfly-style.

2 Lay sardines flesh side uppermost in a ceramic or glass dish with some depth, then pour over vinegar until well covered, cover with a lid or plastic wrap and refrigerate to cure for 24 hours.

3 Carefully remove backbone and separate each sardine into halves lengthways.

4 Lay sardine fillets on the bottom of a clean ceramic or glass dish and sprinkle with garlic, herbs and chilli. Pour over olive oil and refrigerate for 24 hours.

5 Serve with crusty bread that has been topped with tomato and onion. Drizzle over olive oil and sprinkle with more herbs. Garnish with chilli.

**SERVES 10**

# Calamari with Salad of Wild Greens
## Calamari alla griglia con cavolo nero e radicchio

350 g cavolo nero (Tuscan kale), roughly chopped

½ bunch (400 g) chicory, roughly chopped

¼ cup (60 ml) extra virgin olive oil

1 medium brown onion, finely chopped

1 radicchio, roughly chopped

500 g calamari rings

freshly milled sea salt, to taste

freshly ground black pepper, to taste

½ teaspoon chilli flakes

1 egg, lightly beaten

juice of 1 lemon

One of my favourite Italian restaurants in Carlton is Tiamo and my husband Savvas and I have been dining there for almost 30 years. One of our favourite dishes is sautéed calamari in an egg wash (which is gluten free) and this is my version. Try it or visit Tiamo!

1 Boil the cavolo nero with the chicory for 5 minutes, then drain.

2 Heat half the olive oil in a frying pan over medium heat and sauté onion until translucent. Add cooked greens and radicchio, sauté for a few minutes, then transfer to a large platter.

3 Toss calamari in salt, pepper and chilli flakes, and coat in egg. Cook in a frying pan with a little olive oil for 5 minutes, then add to the leaves on the platter.

4 Dress the salad with remaining olive oil and lemon juice, season with salt and pepper, and serve.

SERVES 4

### NUTRIENT COMPOSITION PER SERVE:

| | Average quantity per serving | %RDI ♀ | %RDI ♂ |
|---|---|---|---|
| Energy | 1345 kJ (321 kcal) | 16 | 13 |
| Protein | 26.9 g | 38 | 30 |
| Carbohydrate | 5.8 g | 3 | 2 |
| Total fat | 21.3 g | 24 | 19 |
| Saturated fat | 3.9 g | 28 | 14 |
| Sodium | 425 mg | 27 | 27 |
| Fibre | 6.0 g | 24 | 20 |

# Prawns Saganaki
## Garides saganaki

2 tablespoons extra virgin olive oil

1 red onion, finely chopped

2 cloves garlic, crushed

16–20 large green prawns, heads and tails on, shelled and deveined

½ cup (125 ml) white wine

1 x 400 g can diced Roma tomatoes

½ cup (125 ml) water

1 teaspoon dried mixed herbs

1 small chilli, deseeded (optional) and finely sliced, or ½ teaspoon chilli flakes

2 tablespoons finely chopped fresh flat-leaf parsley

sliced lemon, to serve

1  Heat olive oil in a heavy-based saucepan over medium heat and sauté onion until translucent. Stir through garlic, then add prawns and cook lightly for a few minutes on each side, or until they change colour. Add wine and cook until most of the liquid evaporates. Remove prawns (don't be too fussy if bits of onion and garlic stick to them) and set aside.

2  Add the tomatoes, water, dried herbs and chilli to the sauce. Bring to a boil, then reduce heat and simmer, uncovered, for 15 minutes. Return prawns to the sauce and coat with sauce (taking care not to remove heads).

3  Serve garnished with parsley and sliced lemon.

SERVES 4

NUTRIENT COMPOSITION PER SERVE:

| | Average quantity per serving | %RDI ♀ | ♂ |
|---|---|---|---|
| Energy | 843 kJ (201 kcal) | 10 | 8 |
| Protein | 19.4 g | 27 | 22 |
| Carbohydrate | 5.2 g | 2 | 2 |
| Total fat | 9.9 g | 11 | 9 |
| Saturated fat | 1.7 g | 12 | 6 |
| Sodium | 382 mg | 24 | 24 |
| Fibre | 3.5 g | 14 | 12 |

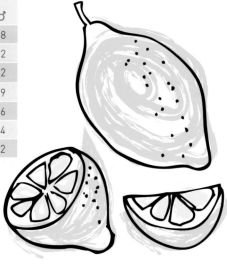

# Fish soup
## Kakavia

⅓ cup (80 ml) olive oil

1 medium onion, finely chopped

1 clove garlic, finely chopped

1 cup (250 ml) puréed tomato or grated tomato
(see page 124)

1 cup (250 ml) white wine

300 g salmon or snapper fillet,
cut into large cubes

4–6 small potatoes, cut into cubes

2 cups (500 ml) fish stock

4–6 large unpeeled green prawns

10–12 mussels

10–12 pipis or clams

200 g cherry tomatoes, cut in half

2 tablespoons chopped fresh flat-leaf parsley

juice of 1 lemon

freshly milled sea salt, to taste

freshly ground black pepper, to taste

**A delicious Greek-style fish soup, high in protein and rich in omega-3 fats.**

**1** Heat olive oil in a large heavy-based stockpot over medium heat and sauté onion until translucent. Add garlic, puréed tomato and wine. Bring to a boil, then reduce heat and simmer, uncovered, for 10 minutes.

**2** Add fish fillet, potato and fish stock, then return to a simmer for 10 minutes. Add prawns and shellfish and simmer for a further 10 minutes.

**3** Just before serving, add cherry tomatoes, parsley and lemon juice, then season with salt and pepper. At this stage, try not to stir pot with a utensil as this may break up the fish. Instead, hold pot by handles and swish soup around.

**SERVES 6**

**NUTRIENT COMPOSITION PER SERVE:**

|  | Average quantity per serving | %RDI ♀ | %RDI ♂ |
|---|---|---|---|
| Energy | 1738 kJ (415 kcal) | 21 | 17 |
| Protein | 40.9 g | 57 | 45 |
| Carbohydrate | 13.6 g | 6 | 5 |
| Total fat | 19.8 g | 22 | 18 |
| Saturated fat | 3.9 g | 28 | 14 |
| Sodium | 673 mg* | 42 | 42 |
| Fibre | 3.1 g | 12 | 10 |

*\* You can lower the sodium content by using salt-reduced stock or homemade stock.*

# Seafood Balls in Egg and Lemon Soup
## Gouvarelakia Thalassina

250 g white fish fillet, minced

250 g prawn meat, minced

1 onion, finely chopped

1 clove garlic, finely chopped

4 spring onions, finely chopped

1 large carrot, grated

1 small fennel bulb, grated

1½ tablespoons extra virgin olive oil

1 cup (200 g) rice

freshly milled sea salt, to taste

freshly ground black pepper, to taste

6 cups (1.5 litres) water

2 eggs, lightly beaten

juice of 2 lemons

**1** In a bowl, mix fish, prawn meat, onion, garlic, spring onions, carrot, fennel, olive oil, rice, salt and pepper until thoroughly combined. Roll small golf-ball-sized pieces of the mixture into balls.

**2** Boil water in a large saucepan, then slowly slip in all the fish balls. Return to a boil, then reduce heat and simmer, uncovered, for 20 minutes.

**3** In a separate bowl, whisk together egg and lemon juice. Take a large spoonful of stock from the fish pot and whisk into egg and lemon, then gradually pour the egg and lemon mixture into the soup and shake pot to stir through.

**4** Serve immediately.

**SERVES 6 (MAKES ABOUT 20 LARGE MEATBALLS)**

### PARTY OPTION

*Roll mixture into balls the size of a large marble, and shallow-fry in olive oil until golden.*

*Serve as finger food with Spicy Saltsa (see page 69).*

**NUTRIENT COMPOSITION PER SERVE:**

| | Average quantity per serving | %RDI ♀ | %RDI ♂ |
|---|---|---|---|
| Energy | 1221 kJ (292 kcal) | 15 | 12 |
| Protein | 22.1 g | 31 | 26 |
| Carbohydrate | 31.3 g | 14 | 11 |
| Total fat | 8.5 g | 9 | 8 |
| Saturated fat | 1.8 g | 13 | 6 |
| Sodium | 220 mg | 14 | 14 |
| Fibre | 2.3 g | 9 | 8 |

# Baked Red Mullet
## Barbounia sto fourno

½ cup (125 ml) extra virgin olive oil

1 red onion, sliced into rings

2 spring onions, sliced

2 bay leaves

1 tablespoon black peppercorns

1 cup (250 ml) white wine

freshly milled sea salt, to taste

freshly ground black pepper, to taste

1 kg red mullet, head and tail on,
  scaled and gutted

½ cup (15 g) finely chopped fresh
  flat-leaf parsley

**Serve this fish with a green salad or a broccoli salad.**

**1** Preheat oven to 180°C.

**2** Heat olive oil in a frying pan over medium heat and sauté onion until translucent. Add spring onions, bay leaves, peppercorns, wine, salt and pepper. Bring to a boil, then reduce heat and simmer for 5 minutes.

**3** Place the mullet in a baking dish. Pour onion marinade over the top and sprinkle with parsley.

**4** Bake for 20–25 minutes, or until fish is cooked.

**5** Transfer to a platter and serve.

**SERVES 6**

### NUTRIENT COMPOSITION PER SERVE:

| | Average quantity per serving | %RDI ♀ | %RDI ♂ |
|---|---|---|---|
| Energy | 1376 kJ (329 kcal) | 17 | 13 |
| Protein | 34.2 g | 48 | 38 |
| Carbohydrate | 1.4 g | 1 | 1 |
| Total fat | 18.7 g | 21 | 17 |
| Saturated fat | 3.7 g | 26 | 13 |
| Sodium | 134 mg | 8 | 8 |
| Fibre | 0.8 g | 3 | 3 |

# Whole Mussels with Rice
## Midorizo

2 tablespoons olive oil

1 medium onion, finely chopped

½ red capsicum, finely chopped

½ green capsicum, finely chopped

½ yellow capsicum, finely chopped

½ teaspoon chilli flakes or 1 fresh chilli, deseeded (optional) and finely sliced

1 cup (200 g) rice

1½ cups (375 ml) water

1 cup (250 ml) white wine

1 kg mussels

freshly milled sea salt, to taste

freshly ground black pepper, to taste

2 tablespoons chopped fresh flat-leaf parsley

My cousin Noula Karakostantinou from Northern Greece has perfected this recipe of fresh mussels with rice and the vegetable favourite of Northern Greeks, colourful capsicum.

**1** Heat olive oil in a large heavy-based saucepan over medium heat and sauté onion, capsicum, and chilli flakes until onion is translucent and capsicum is soft. Add rice and cook, stirring frequently, until rice starts to become translucent. Add water, bring to a boil, then reduce heat and simmer for 5 minutes, or until rice is almost cooked.

**2** In a separate saucepan, pour wine over mussels. Bring to a boil, then reduce heat and simmer until mussels open.

**3** Stir mussels and wine through rice mixture, then cook for a few minutes, or until most of the liquid has evaporated and rice is cooked through.

**4** Season with salt and pepper, garnish with parsley, and serve.

**SERVES 4**

## NUTRIENT COMPOSITION PER SERVE

|  | Average quantity per serving | %RDI ♀ | %RDI ♂ |
|---|---|---|---|
| Energy | 1421 kJ (339 kcal) | 17 | 14 |
| Protein | 10.9 g | 15 | 12 |
| Carbohydrate | 43.3 g | 19 | 15 |
| Total fat | 10.5 g | 12 | 10 |
| Saturated fat | 1.9 g | 13 | 7 |
| Sodium | 220 mg | 14 | 14 |
| Fibre | 1.6 g | 7 | 5 |

# Mussel and Prawn Pilafi
## Pilafi me midia

2 kg mussels

¼ cup (60 ml) olive oil

1 bunch (200 g) spring onions

2 cups (400 g) rice

1 kg shelled green prawns, deveined (optional)

1 cup (30 g) finely chopped fresh flat-leaf parsley

freshly milled sea salt, to taste

freshly ground black pepper, to taste

**NUTRIENT COMPOSITION PER SERVE:**

| | Average quantity per serving | %RDI ♀ | ♂ |
|---|---|---|---|
| Energy | 2185 kJ (522 kcal) | 27 | 21 |
| Protein | 46.5 g | 65 | 52 |
| Carbohydrate | 56.5 g | 24 | 20 |
| Total fat | 11.7 g | 13 | 11 |
| Saturated fat | 2.3 g | 16 | 8 |
| Sodium | 816 mg | 51 | 51 |
| Fibre | 1.3 g | 5 | 4 |

A favourite family meal of my friend Helen Karikas, created by her mother Vasiliki Patsakos. Vasiliki is married to a fisherman Yiannis who regularly brings home fresh mussels and calamari.

**1** Add enough water to cover mussels in a saucepan, then bring to a boil. Reduce heat and simmer until the mussels open, then set aside in water until cool. Drain, reserving 600 ml stock. Remove mussels from shells, discarding shells.

**2** Heat olive oil in a heavy-based saucepan and sauté spring onion until translucent.

**3** Add rice and cook, stirring frequently, until rice starts to become translucent. Add prawns and move around until cooked through. Stir through parsley and cook for 1 minute. Add mussels and stir through.

**4** Add reserved stock and 2 cups (500 ml) water, then bring to a boil. Reduce heat and simmer, covered, for 15–20 minutes, or until rice is cooked. Add more water during cooking if necessary.

**5** Season with salt and pepper, then serve.

**SERVES 6–8**

# Pearl Barley Risotto with Zucchini and Prawns
## Risotto con orzo perlato con zucchine e gamberetti

¼ cup (60 ml) olive oil

1 medium onion

1 clove garlic, finely chopped

16–20 medium shelled green prawns, deveined,
  each cut into 3 pieces

1 medium zucchini, thinly sliced

2 cups (400 g) pearl barley, soaked overnight
  in cold water

½ cup (125 ml) white wine

4 cups (1 litre) hot fish stock

hot water, as needed

½ cup (15 g) finely chopped fresh
  flat-leaf parsley

freshly milled sea salt, to taste

freshly ground black pepper, to taste

juice of ½ lemon

**1** Heat olive oil in a frying pan over medium heat and sauté onion until translucent. Stir through garlic, then add prawns and cook for 3–4 minutes. Remove prawns (don't be too fussy if bits of onion and garlic stick to them) and keep warm in shallow dish covered with aluminium foil.

**2** Add zucchini to the same frying pan and sauté lightly. Add pearl barley and wine, then stir for 3–4 minutes, or until wine has evaporated.

**3** Add about half a cup of fish stock and stir until almost absorbed, then add another half-cup of stock and stir until almost absorbed. Continue adding stock in this way until all stock has been used. Check pearl barley. If not cooked through, gradually add hot water in the same way until barley is cooked.

**4** Return prawns to the pan, then add parsley, and season with salt and pepper. Sprinkle over lemon juice and serve.

**SERVES 6**

### NUTRIENT COMPOSITION PER SERVE:

| | Average quantity per serving | %RDI ♀ | %RDI ♂ |
|---|---|---|---|
| Energy | 1526 kJ (365 kcal) | 19 | 15 |
| Protein | 18.9 g | 26 | 21 |
| Carbohydrate | 43.2 g | 19 | 15 |
| Total fat | 11.8 g | 13 | 11 |
| Saturated fat | 2.0 g | 14 | 7 |
| Sodium | 857 mg | 54 | 54 |
| Fibre | 8.6 g | 34 | 29 |

# Biscuits and Sweets

## Biskota kai Gluka

# Chewy Almond Biscuits
## Amigdalota

3 egg whites

1½ cups (330 g) caster sugar

3 cups (300 g) almond meal

1 teaspoon mastiha paste or ground gum mastic

1 tablespoon amaretto or Frangelico

1½ cups (150 g) almond flakes

### NUTRIENT COMPOSITION PER BISCUIT:

| | Quantity per serve | %RDI ♀ | %RDI ♂ |
|---|---|---|---|
| Energy | 778 kJ (186 kcal) | 9 | 8 |
| Protein | 4.8 g | 7 | 5 |
| Carbohydrate | 15.8 g | 7 | 6 |
| Total fat | 11.7 g | 13 | 11 |
| Saturated fat | 0.7 g | 5 | 3 |
| Sodium | 9 mg | 1 | 1 |
| Fibre | 1.9 g | 8 | 6 |

**These delicious chewy almond biscuits are easy to make and are gluten free.**

**1** Preheat oven to 180°C and line 2 baking trays with baking paper.

**2** Beat the egg whites in a medium bowl until soft peaks form. Add sugar and continue beating until mixture is thick and shiny.

**3** In a large bowl, combine the almond meal, mastiha paste and amaretto. Fold the egg white mixture into the almond mixture.

**4** Roll walnut-size pieces of dough into balls then roll in almond flakes (or alternatively, mix flaked almonds into dough before rolling for an all-through crunch). Place on prepared baking trays, leaving a few centimetres around each biscuit – they do spread a little.

**5** Bake for 16–18 minutes, or until golden. Allow to cool on trays over a wire rack. They will be very soft when they come out of the oven but will harden as they cool.

**MAKES 20–25 BISCUITS**

# Mary's Easter Bread
## Tsoureki

60 g fresh yeast, crumbled, or 1½ tablespoons (3 × 7 g sachets) dried yeast

2 cups (500 ml) lukewarm milk

10⅔ cups (1.6 kg) farina flour, sifted

250 g unsalted butter, melted

2½ cups (275 g) caster sugar

6 eggs, plus extra 1 egg for glazing

1 tablespoon mahlepi (a Greek spice)

1½ tablespoons vanillin sugar

red-dyed eggs, to decorate (optional)

flaked almonds, to decorate (optional)

### NUTRIENT COMPOSITION PER 80 G SLICE:

|  | Quantity per serve | %RDI | |
|---|---|---|---|
|  |  | ♀ | ♂ |
| Energy | 849 kJ (203 kcal) | 10 | 8 |
| Protein | 4.6 g | 6 | 5 |
| Carbohydrate | 34.4 g | 15 | 12 |
| Total fat | 5.3 g | 6 | 5 |
| Saturated fat | 3.1 g | 22 | 11 |
| Sodium | 234 mg | 15 | 15 |
| Fibre | 1.3 g | 5 | 4 |

Tsoureki, a sweet yeast bread made of eggs, milk and butter, is a staple during Greek Easter and is made to break the Lenten fast. The three-strand braid symbolises the Holy Trinity, while the red-dyed hard-boiled egg braided into the dough symbolises the blood of Christ.

I grew up in a Greek household and Easter was the most important celebration of the year. Everyone made something that symbolised Easter, such as painting boiled eggs red, making Easter biscuits, or making tsoureki. My dear friend Mary Amiridis has perfected the art of tsoureki making, and this is her recipe.

1  Add yeast to milk and dissolve well. Mix in 2¼ cups (340 g) of the flour, then cover and leave in a warm place for about 1 hour, or until dough doubles in size.

2  Beat together butter and sugar for 15–20 minutes, or until mixture becomes creamy and light. Slowly add eggs one by one, beating well after each addition. Add mahlepi and vanillin sugar, and beat until combined.

3  Add egg and sugar mixture to the yeast preparation and mix gently. Slowly fold remaining flour into the mixture until it forms a smooth dough.

4  Line a large baking sheet with baking paper. Roll dough into logs and mould into shapes (such as plaits, twists, wreaths) and place on prepared baking sheet, then cover and leave in a warm place for 2–3 hours, or until doubled in size.

5  Preheat oven to 160°C.

6  Glaze dough with extra beaten egg. Place red-dyed eggs in the centre and sprinkle over flaked almonds, if using. Bake for 20 minutes, or until golden brown and cooked through. Tsoureki is cooked when a knife or skewer inserted in the centre comes out clean.

# Vasiliki's Vasilopita

⅓ cup (80 ml) olive oil

75 g butter, melted

1 × 375 g packet (18–20 sheets) filo pastry

180 g almonds, toasted in a dry frying pan,
   crushed

350 g walnuts, crushed

130 g sesame seeds, toasted in a dry frying pan,
   lightly ground

1 teaspoon mastiha (gum mastic), ground

1 teaspoon vanillin sugar

¾ cup (165 g) caster sugar

3 teaspoons ground cinnamon

blanched almonds, to decorate


**SYRUP**

1 cup (220 g) sugar

1 cup (250 ml) water

**A baklava with a difference. This traditional dessert is made in the North of Greece for New Year's Eve celebrations. It is a recipe from Vasiliki Patsakos, the mother of my friend Helen Karikas.**

**1** Preheat oven to 180°C and grease a 30 cm round cake tin.

**2** Mix olive oil with melted butter in a small bowl. Take a sheet of filo pastry and brush with butter mixture, then fold in half and place in the bottom of prepared cake tin. Repeat with a second sheet of filo pastry.

**3** Mix the almonds, walnuts, sesame seeds, mastiha, vanillin sugar, caster sugar and cinnamon in a bowl. Ruche 2 filo pastry sheets and place on top of second layer, then brush with olive oil and butter mixture and sprinkle with a little of the nut mixture.

**4** Repeat the last step, ruching pairs of filo sheets and sprinkling with nuts, until all but 2 filo pastry sheets are used.

**5** Brush the final 2 sheets with butter mixture and cut into 30 cm rounds. Place neatly on top of cake. Decorate with blanched almonds and sprinkle a little water on top. Cut slits into top with a sharp knife.

**6** Bake for 30 minutes or until golden.

**7** Meanwhile, make a sugar syrup by stirring sugar into water in a small saucepan and warming over medium heat until sugar dissolves. Increase heat and bring to a boil, then reduce heat and simmer for 10 minutes, or until syrup thickens slightly. When cake is ready, pour cooled syrup over the cake and allow to stand until syrup is absorbed.

**8** Using a sharp knife, cut into wedges or small squares.

**SERVES 12**

## NUTRIENT COMPOSITION PER 150 G PIECE:

|  | Quantity per serve | %RDI | |
|---|---|---|---|
|  |  | ♀ | ♂ |
| Energy | 2793 kJ (667 kcal) | 34 | 27 |
| Protein | 12.6 g | 18 | 14 |
| Carbohydrate | 52.2 g | 23 | 18 |
| Total fat | 46.5 g | 52 | 42 |
| Saturated fat | 7.0 g | 50 | 25 |
| Sodium | 230 mg | 14 | 14 |
| Fibre | 5.7 g | 23 | 19 |

# Figs Stuffed with Ricotta, Honey and Walnuts
## Gemista sika me rikota kai meli

**300 g mascapone or ricotta**

**½ cup (125 ml) honey, plus extra for drizzling**

**½ teaspoon ground nutmeg, plus extra for sprinkling**

**¼ cup (30 g) crushed walnuts**

**¼ cup (30 g) crushed hazelnuts**

**12 fresh figs**

**1** Mix mascapone with honey, nutmeg and half of each of the nuts.

**2** Cut a cross into the top of each fig, and pinch them open. Fill each fig with the cheese and honey mixture.

**3** Sprinkle over extra nutmeg and remaining hazelnuts and walnuts. Serve with a little drizzle of honey.

**SERVES 6**

### NUTRIENT COMPOSITION PER SERVE:

|  | Quantity per serve | %RDI ♀ | %RDI ♂ |
|---|---|---|---|
| Energy | 1147 kJ (274 kcal) | 14 | 11 |
| Protein | 7.7 g | 11 | 9 |
| Carbohydrate | 37.0 g | 16 | 13 |
| Total fat | 11.3 g | 13 | 10 |
| Saturated fat | 2.9 g | 21 | 10 |
| Sodium | 68 mg | 4 | 4 |
| Fibre | 5.2 g | 21 | 17 |

# Baked Custard Pie with Filo Pastry
## Bougatsa

4 cups (1 litre) milk

1 cup (125 g) fine semolina

250 g unsalted butter

grated zest and juice of ½ lemon

4 eggs

1 cup (220 g) caster sugar

2 teaspoons vanillin sugar

2 tablespoons olive oil

10 sheets filo pastry

### NUTRIENT COMPOSITION PER 180 G SERVE:

| | Quantity per serve | %RDI ♀ | %RDI ♂ |
|---|---|---|---|
| Energy | 1767 kJ (422 kcal) | 21 | 17 |
| Protein | 8.0 g | 11 | 9 |
| Carbohydrate | 43.2 g | 19 | 15 |
| Total fat | 24.8 g | 28 | 23 |
| Saturated fat | 13.9 | 99 | 50 |
| Sodium | 278 mg | 17 | 17 |
| Fibre | 0.9 g | 4 | 3 |

This classic Greek custard-based pastry which is served warm with a dusting of cinnamon makes a perfect dessert for a dinner party. Pre-prepare the bougatsa pie and bake straight after dinner so it can be enjoyed warm and freshly baked. Recipe kindly provided by Helen Karikas.

**1** Preheat oven to 200°C and grease a low-sided cake tin (rectangular or 30 cm round).

**2** In a large saucepan, heat milk gently over medium heat until almost boiling, then slowly add semolina, stirring constantly. Bring to a boil and keep stirring until the mixture thickens to consistency of thin porridge (about 5 minutes).

**3** Add half the butter, and the lemon zest and juice, stir until the butter is melted, then remove from heat and set aside to cool until lukewarm

**4** Beat eggs, sugar and vanillin sugar until creamy. Slowly add beaten egg mixture to cooled semolina mixture, whisking until well combined.

**5** Melt remaining butter with olive oil. One sheet at a time, brush filo pastry sheets with butter mixture and place on bottom of prepared cake tin. Repeat until you have layered 5 sheets of filo in the tin. Pour semolina custard into pan. Brush each of the remaining 5 filo sheets with butter mixture then layer on top of custard. Fold over the bottom layers of filo to seal in the pie.

**6** Bake for 30–40 minutes, or until top is golden brown and custard is cooked through.

**7** Allow to cool for 10 minutes. Using a sharp knife, cut into squares and serve with ice cream and a sprinkle of icing sugar or cinnamon.

**SERVES 12**

# Greek Doughnuts
## Loukoumades

2 cups (500 ml) lukewarm water

½ teaspoon salt

1 tablespoon white vinegar

½ teaspoon sugar

2 teaspoons (1 × 7 g sachet) dried yeast

3⅓ cups (500 g) plain flour

½ teaspoon baking powder

oil, for deep-frying

½ cup (125 ml) honey

½ cup crushed walnuts

½ teaspoon ground cinnamon

ice cream, to serve

My mother-in-law Paraskevi Koutsis is known for her loukoumades. Crispy hot sweet doughnut balls coated with honey and dusted with crushed walnuts and cinnamon are just the ideal treat after a Greek feast.

**1** Pour lukewarm water into a large bowl and stir in salt, vinegar, sugar and yeast until sugar and yeast dissolve.

**2** Beating constantly at first, slowly add sifted flour and baking powder. Cover bowl and set aside in a warm place for 90 minutes, or until dough doubles in size.

**3** In a large, heavy-based pan, heat oil for deep-frying. Working in batches, break off small pieces of dough and roll into balls, then slide them gently into hot oil, taking care not to splash yourself, and fry until golden. Remove from oil using a slotted metal spoon and drain on kitchen paper while cooking the next batch. When all are cooked, transfer to a large bowl.

**4** Heat honey in a small saucepan over medium heat until it starts frothing. Remove from heat and pour over the cooked loukoumades. Sprinkle over walnuts, dust with cinnamon and serve with ice cream.

**MAKES ABOUT 25 DOUGHNUTS**

### NUTRIENT COMPOSITION PER 3-DOUGHNUT SERVE:

| | Quantity per serve | %RDI ♀ | ♂ |
|---|---|---|---|
| Energy | 1509 kJ (360 kcal) | 6 | 5 |
| Protein | 6.9 g | 3 | 3 |
| Carbohydrate | 61.8 g | 9 | 7 |
| Total fat | 9.6 g | 4 | 3 |
| Saturated fat | 1.5 g | 4 | 2 |
| Sodium | 231 mg | 5 | 5 |
| Fibre | 2.4 g | 3 | 3 |

# Yoghurt Cake
## Yiaourtopita

1 cup (250 ml) olive oil or 250 g unsalted butter, softened

1½ cups (330 g) caster sugar

1 cup (260 g) Greek-style yoghurt, plus extra to serve

5 eggs, separated

2 teaspoons grated lemon zest

2 teaspoons grated lime zest

3 cups (450 g) self-raising flour

1 teaspoon baking powder

1 teaspoon ground cinnamon, plus extra for dusting

**SYRUP**

1 cup (250 ml) water

½ cup (125 ml) lemon juice

1½ cups (330 g) sugar

zest of 1 lemon (or lime)

1 stick cinnamon

**1** Preheat oven to 180°C and grease a round cake tin.

**2** Beat olive oil and sugar for 5 minutes, or until creamy. Add yoghurt and beat until combined. Add egg yolks and grated lemon and lime zests, then continue beating for a few minutes, or until thoroughly combined.

**3** In a separate bowl, beat egg whites until soft peaks form. Slowly fold egg whites into cake mixture, then gradually fold in sifted flour, baking powder and cinnamon.

**4** Pour mixture into prepared cake tin and bake for 1 hour, or until a skewer inserted into the middle of the cake comes out clean.

**5** While cake is baking, make syrup by combining ingredients in a saucepan and heat over low heat until sugar dissolves and just starts to bubble, remove cinnamon stick – remove from heat and cool.

**6** Remove cake from pan while still hot and place on a large plate with a lip. Pour over cooled syrup (one of either the cake or the syrup should be hot and the other cold for best effect).

**7** Serve with a scoop of yoghurt and dusted with cinnamon.

**SERVES 10**

**NUTRIENT COMPOSITION PER 150 G SERVE:**

| | Quantity per serve | %RDI ♀ | %RDI ♂ |
|---|---|---|---|
| Energy | 2234 kJ (534 kcal) | 27 | 22 |
| Protein | 8.8 g | 12 | 10 |
| Carbohydrate | 63.9 g | 28 | 22 |
| Total fat | 27.7 g | 31 | 25 |
| Saturated fat | 6.0 g | 43 | 22 |
| Sodium | 529 mg | 33 | 33 |
| Fibre | 1.8 g | 7 | 6 |

# Hazelnut Biscotti

1¾ cups (260 g) self-raising flour

1 cup (135 g) roasted hazelnuts, skins off,
roughly chopped

1 teaspoon baking powder

¼ teaspoon salt

3 eggs

1 teaspoon vanilla extract

1 cup (220 g) firmly packed brown sugar

1 shot (30 ml) strong espresso coffee

### NUTRIENT COMPOSITION PER BISCUIT:

| | Quantity per serve | %RDI ♀ | ♂ |
|---|---|---|---|
| Energy | 565 kJ (135 kcal) | 7 | 6 |
| Protein | 3.2 g | 5 | 4 |
| Carbohydrate | 18.9 g | 8 | 7 |
| Total fat | 5.3 g | 6 | 5 |
| Saturated fat | 0.4 g | 3 | 2 |
| Sodium | 258 mg | 16 | 16 |
| Fibre | 1.2 g | 5 | 4 |

**An Italian favourite enjoyed with a shot of espresso coffee.**

**1** Preheat oven to 180°C and line a baking tray with baking paper.

**2** Sift flour and combine with hazelnuts, baking powder and salt.

**3** Beat eggs with vanilla extract, brown sugar and coffee, then mix into flour mixture until a dough forms. Divide dough into 2 pieces and shape each into a long loaf (similar to a ciabatta loaf).

**4** Place on prepared baking tray, leaving space between loaves, and bake for 30 minutes. The dough will still be soft.

**5** Reduce oven to 150°C.

**6** Allow loaves to cool sufficiently for you to cut them into 1 cm slices. Working in batches if necessary, return slices to baking tray and bake for 20 minutes (turning halfway through cooking), or until biscuits are crisp.

**MAKES 20–25 BISCUITS**

# Chestnut, Almond and Fig Cake
## Keik me kastana kai sika

1 cup (95 g) chestnut flour

1 teaspoon baking powder

1 cup (100 g) almond meal

¼ teaspoon ground cinnamon plus extra
  for sprinkling

3 eggs, separated

½ cup (125 ml) olive oil

½ cup (125 ml) honey

⅓ cup (80 g) caster sugar

8–9 (100 g) dried figs, soaked in lukewarm water
  for 30 minutes to soften, then drained and
  minced or finely chopped

1–2 tablespoons cognac

½ teaspoon salt

### ORANGE SYRUP

½ cup (125 ml) fresh orange juice

½ cup (110 g) caster sugar

½ cup (125 ml) water

This warm moist cake has a nutty flavour and is perfect served with Greek-style yoghurt and a strong coffee. It is also gluten free.

**1** Preheat oven to 180°C.

**2** Sift chestnut flour with baking powder and stir through almond meal. Add cinnamon.

**3** Beat egg yolks with olive oil, honey and half the sugar for 5 minutes. Fold through minced figs. Fold through flour mixture until completely incorporated. Add cognac and mix through well.

**4** In a separate bowl, beat egg whites with salt, then slowly add remaining sugar until soft peaks form. Gradually fold egg whites into egg yolk and flour mixture until well combined.

**5** Pour into prepared cake tin and bake for 30 minutes, then cover with aluminium foil and cook for another 5–10 minutes, or until a skewer inserted into the middle of the cake comes out clean.

**6** Serve with an orange syrup made with fresh orange juice, caster sugar and water. Place in a small saucepan and stir over low heat for about 10 minutes until thickened slightly, then set aside to cool.

**7** Serve cake warm, drizzled with orange syrup and a dollop of Greek-style yoghurt with a sprinkle of cinnamon.

SERVES 8

**NUTRIENT COMPOSITION PER 120 G SERVE:**

|  | Quantity per serve | %RDI ♀ | %RDI ♂ |
|---|---|---|---|
| Energy | 1713 kJ (409 kcal) | 21 | 17 |
| Protein | 6.1 g | 9 | 7 |
| Carbohydrate | 41.3 g | 18 | 14 |
| Total fat | 24.3 g | 27 | 22 |
| Saturated fat | 3.5 g | 24 | 12 |
| Sodium | 415 mg | 26 | 26 |
| Fibre | 5.7 g | 23 | 19 |

# Cherry Spoon Sweets
## Kerasi Gluko tou Koutaliou

1 kg cherries

2 cups (440 g) sugar

½ cup (125 ml) water

1 tablespoon lemon juice

**NUTRIENT COMPOSITION PER
5-CHERRY (40 G) SERVE:**

|  | Quantity per serve | %RDI ♀ | %RDI ♂ |
|---|---|---|---|
| Energy | 220 kJ (53 kcal) | 3 | 2 |
| Protein | 0.2 g | 0 | 0 |
| Carbohydrate | 13.3 g | 6 | 5 |
| Total fat | 0 g | 0 | 0 |
| Saturated fat | 0 g | 0 | 0 |
| Sodium | <1 mg | 0 | 0 |
| Fibre | 0.4 g | 2 | 1 |

**Each summer when the cherries are in season, my husband buys a 5 kg box and drops it off to my mother Theano so she can make this sweet, which Savvas enjoys drizzled over ice cream throughout the year.**

**1** Pit cherries and put them in a medium saucepan. Add sugar, water and lemon juice, then stir gently, taking care not to break up the cherries. Warm over medium heat until just boiling, then reduce heat and simmer, uncovered, until the liquid forms a thick syrup. As the cherries are simmering, remove and discard any foam that collects on top.

**2** Test whether the syrup is thick enough by removing a small amount with a teaspoon and dropping a little onto a plate. If a small ball forms, the syrup is ready.

**3** Remove from heat and allow to cool, then transfer to sterilised jars with well-fitting lids. The sweets will keep for up to 1 year in the refrigerator.

**4** Serve 1–2 teaspoons of sweet on a small plate accompanied with a glass of cold water. (Alternatively, drizzle over ice cream for a delicious dessert.)

# Baked Quince
## Kidoni sto fourno me koniak kai foundoukia

2 large or 4 small quinces

¼ cup (60 ml) brandy (we use Metaxa 5 Star)

½ cup (125 ml) honey

½ teaspoon cinnamon, plus extra to serve

¼ cup (40 g) hazelnuts, crushed

4–5 dried figs, soaked in lukewarm water for
   30 minutes to soften, then drained and chopped

thick Greek-style yoghurt, to serve

**1** Preheat oven to 150°C and grease a baking dish.

**2** Scrub quinces to remove outer fur, then cut in quarters,
and place in prepared dish.

**3** Mix brandy with honey and pour over quince. Sprinkle over
cinnamon, hazelnuts and figs.

**4** Cover dish with aluminium foil and bake for 90 minutes,
or until quinces have caramelised and turned deep orange.

**5** Serve warm, with a dollop of yoghurt and sprinkled with
cinnamon.

**SERVES 6**

### SERVING SIZE: 150 G

| | Quantity per serve | %RDI ♀ | %RDI ♂ |
|---|---|---|---|
| Energy | 1050 kJ (251 kcal) | 13 | 10 |
| Protein | 1.7 g | 3 | 2 |
| Carbohydrate | 44.5 g | 19 | 16 |
| Total fat | 3.3 g | 4 | 3 |
| Saturated fat | 0.2 g | 1 | 1 |
| Sodium | 18 mg | 1 | 1 |
| Fibre | 5.0 g | 20 | 17 |

# Apples Poached in Red Wine
## Mila pose se kokkino krasi

2–3 apples, peeled and quartered

2 cups (500 ml) red wine

⅓ cup (80 g) caster sugar (if using a sweeter wine use less sugar or omit)

1 teaspoon ground nutmeg, plus extra for sprinkling

thick Greek-style yoghurt, to serve

¼ cup (25 g) flaked almonds, to serve

**My dad always used to finish his evening meal with an apple he carefully peeled and quartered and then shared with the family. He always placed his quarter in a glass of red wine and enjoyed it later when it was steeped in wine and had turned a bright burgundy colour.**

1  Put apples, wine, sugar and nutmeg in a medium saucepan over medium heat and bring to a boil, then reduce heat and simmer for 30 minutes. Carefully remove apples using a slotted spoon and set aside. Continue to simmer wine until it is reduced by half.

2  Serve apples in shallow bowl with red wine syrup drizzled over and a dollop of thick Greek-style yoghurt. Sprinkle with flaked almonds and a little nutmeg.

**SERVES 6**

### NUTRIENT COMPOSITION PER SERVE:

|  | Quantity per serve | %RDI ♀ | ♂ |
|---|---|---|---|
| Energy | 674 kJ (161 kcal) | 8 | 7 |
| Protein | 1.9 g | 3 | 2 |
| Carbohydrate | 20.9 g | 9 | 7 |
| Total fat | 4.0 g | 4 | 4 |
| Saturated fat | 0.3 g | 2 | 1 |
| Sodium | 10 mg | 1 | 1 |
| Fibre | 2.2 g | 9 | 7 |

# Chewy Fruit and Nut Bars
## Pasteli me amigdala kai apoxiramena frouta

1 cup (500 ml) honey

2 cups (290 g) sesame seeds

²⁄₃ cup (100 g) raw almonds

²⁄₃ cup (100 g) dried berries (cranberries, blueberries, blackcurrants)

1 teaspoon ground cinnamon

**A tasty and healthy high-fibre snack that's perfect for school, uni or work.**

1 Line a 20 x 30 cm lamington tin with baking paper.

2 Heat honey in a small saucepan over medium heat until it just starts to bubble. Remove from heat.

3 Combine the seeds and almonds and toast in another dry heavy-based saucepan over low heat for 5 minutes, or until sesame seeds start to brown. Add berries and cinnamon and continue to toast for a few minutes.

4 Pour hot honey into seed mixture and stir for 2–3 minutes, or until mixture starts to stick to spoon.

5 Pour into prepared tray, place another layer of baking paper over the top, then roll flat with a rolling pin and remove top layer of paper.

6 Allow to cool thoroughly, then cut into 2 x 5 cm rectangles. Store in an airtight container with sheets of baking paper between layers to prevent them sticking together.

**MAKES 20 BARS**

### NUTRIENT COMPOSITION PER 50 G BAR:

|  | Quantity per serve | %RDI | |
|---|---|---|---|
|  |  | ♀ | ♂ |
| Energy | 828 kJ (198 kcal) | 10 | 8 |
| Protein | 4.5 g | 6 | 5 |
| Carbohydrate | 21.6 g | 9 | 7 |
| Total fat | 11.1 g | 12 | 10 |
| Saturated fat | 1.2 g | 9 | 4 |
| Sodium | 9 mg | 1 | 1 |
| Fibre | 2.3 g | 9 | 8 |

# Paximadia Biscuits
## Paximadia nistisima

1 cup (250 ml) olive oil

½ cup (110 g) sugar

½ cup (125 ml) fresh orange juice

5 cups (750 g) self-raising flour

1 tablespoon ground cinnamon

½ tablespoon baking powder

1 tablespoon sesame seeds

A traditional Greek dairy-free sweet biscuit that is often made during fasting periods as it is totally vegan. I thank Vasilika Barbounis for this recipe.

**1** Preheat oven to 180°C and line 2 baking sheets with baking paper.

**2** Beat oil with sugar and orange juice for 10 minutes, or until creamy. Stir in sifted flour, cinnamon and baking powder until mixture forms a soft dough. Divide dough into 2 pieces, then roll each piece into a small loaf. Sprinkle loaves with sesame seeds.

**3** Bake for 15 minutes, turn biscuits over, cook for another 15 minutes. Remove from oven and cool loaves for 10 minutes. Cut into 1.5–2.0 cm slices and place on baking tray. Bake for another 10–15 minutes until biscuits are crisp.

**MAKES 50 BISCUITS**

### NUTRIENT COMPOSITION PER 40 G BISCUIT:

| | Quantity per serve | %RDI ♀ | %RDI ♂ |
|---|---|---|---|
| Energy | 647 kJ (155 kcal) | 8 | 6 |
| Protein | 3.2 g | 5 | 4 |
| Carbohydrate | 24.2 g | 11 | 8 |
| Total fat | 4.9 g | 6 | 5 |
| Saturated fat | 0.8 g | 6 | 3 |
| Sodium | 75 mg | 5 | 5 |
| Fibre | 1.3 g | 5 | 4 |

# REFERENCES

Anton, S. & Leeuwenburgh, C. (2013) 'Fasting or caloric restriction for healthy aging', *Experimental Gerontology*, vol. 48, no. 10, pp. 1003–1005.

Bach-Faig A. et al. (2011) 'Mediterranean diet pyramid today: science and cultural updates', *Public Health and Nutrition*, vol. 14, no. 12A, pp. 2274–84.

Barnosky, A.R. et al. (2014) 'Intermittent fasting vs daily calorie restriction for type 2 diabetes prevention: a review of human findings', *Translational Research*, vol. 164, no. 4, pp. 302–11.

Bezerra, I.N. et al. (2012) 'Association between eating out of home and body weight', *Nutrition Reviews*, vol. 70, no. 2, pp. 65–79.

Clarke, J.D. et al. (2011) 'Differential effects of sulforaphane on histone deacetylases, cell cycle arrest and apoptosis in normal prostate cells versus hyperplastic and cancerous prostate cells', *Molecular Nutrition and Food Research*, vol. 55, no. 7, pp. 999–1009.

Constant J. (1997) 'Alcohol, ischaemic heart disease, and the French paradox', *Clinical Cardiology*, vol. 20, no. 5, pp. 420–24.

Crous-Bou, M. et al. (2014) 'Mediterranean diet and telomere length in Nurses' Health Study: population based cohort study', *British Medical Journal*, vol. 349: g6674, www.bmj.com/content/349/bmj.g6674.

Darmadi-Blackberry, I. et al. (2004) 'Legumes: the most important dietary predictor of survival in older people of different ethnicities', *Asia Pacific Journal of Clinical Nutrition*, vol. 13, no. 2, pp. 217–20, apjcn.nhri.org.tw/server/info/articles/diets-foods/Darmadi.pdf.

Donato A.J. et al. (2015) 'Cellular and molecular biology of aging endothelial cells', *Journal of Molecular and Cellular Cardiology*, pii: S0022–2828(15)00034–6.

Duffey, K.J. et al. (2007) 'Differential associations of fast food and restaurant food consumption with 3-y change in body mass index: the Coronary Artery Risk Development in Young Adults Study', *American Journal of Clinical Nutrition*, vol. 85, no. 1, pp. 201–208.

Dymiotis, M. (2014) 'Food, memories, and pleasure: grandmother's practices', *Food Studies*, vol. 5, no. 1, pp. 19–30.

Eaton S.B. & M. Konner (1985) 'Paleolithic nutrition: a consideration of its nature and current implications', *New England Journal of Medicine*, vol. 312, no. 5, pp. 283–89.

Fardet, A. & Y. Boirie (2014) 'Associations between food and beverage groups and major diet-related chronic diseases: an exhaustive review of pooled/meta-analyses and systematic reviews', *Nutrition Reviews*, vol. 72, no. 12, pp. 741–62.

Fielding, J.M. et al. (2005) 'Increases in plasma lycopene concentration after consumption of tomatoes cooked with olive oil', *Asia Pacific Journal of Clinical Nutrition*, vol. 14, no. 2, pp. 131–36.

Giacosa, A. et al. (2014) 'Mediterranean way of drinking and longevity', *Critical Reviews in Food Science and Nutrition*, doi: 10.1080/10408398.2012.747484.

Giovannucci, E. et al. (2003) 'A prospective study of cruciferous vegetables and prostate cancer', *Cancer Epidemiology, Biomarkers and Prevention*, vol. 12, no. 12, pp. 1403–409.

Harvie M. et al. (2011) 'The effects of intermittent or continuous energy restriction on weight loss and metabolic disease risk markers: a randomised trial in young overweight women', *International Journal of Obesity* (London), vol. 35, no. 5, pp. 714–27.

Hursting, S.D. et al. (2003) 'Calorie restriction, aging, and cancer prevention: mechanisms of action and applicability to humans', *Annual Review of Medicine*, vol. 54, pp. 131–52.

Itsiopoulos, C. et al. (2009) 'Can the Mediterranean diet prevent prostate cancer?' *Molecular Nutrition and Food Research*, vol. 53, no. 2, pp. 227–39.

Johnson R.J. et al. (2013) 'Sugar, uric acid, and the etiology of diabetes and obesity', *Diabetes*, vol. 62, no. 10, pp. 3307–15.

Kapiszewska, M. et al. (2005) 'The estrogenic status and the COMT genotype of female blood donors influence the protective ability of the Mediterranean plant extracts against the hydrogen peroxide-induced DNA damage in lymphocytes', *Journal of Physiology and Pharmacology*, vol. 56, suppl. 1, pp. 199–217.

Keys, A. (1970) 'Coronary heart disease in seven countries', *Circulation*, vol. 41, suppl. 1, pp. 1–211.

Kouris-Blazos A. & C. Itsiopoulos (2014) 'Low all-cause mortality despite high cardiovascular risk in elderly Greek-born Australians: attenuating potential of diet?', *Asia Pacific Journal of Clinical Nutrition*, vol. 23, no. 4, pp. 532–44, apjcn.nhri.org.tw/server/APJCN/23/4/532.pdf.

Krishnan, S. et al. (2010) 'Consumption of restaurant foods and incidence of type 2 diabetes in African American women', *American Journal of Clinical Nutrition*, vol. 91, no. 2, pp. 465–71.

Lim EL, et al, (2011) 'Reversal of type 2 diabetes: normalisation of beta cell function in association with decreased pancreas and liver triacylglycerol, Diabetologia. vol. 54, no. 10, pp. 2506-14.

Longo, V.D. & M.P. Mattson (2014) 'Fasting: molecular mechanisms and clinical applications', *Cell Metabolism*, vol. 19, no. 2, pp. 181–92.

Lucas, L. et al. (2011) 'Molecular mechanisms of inflammation: anti-inflammatory benefits of virgin olive oil and the phenolic compound oleocanthal', *Current Pharmaceutical Design*, vol. 17, no. 8, pp. 754–68.

McLachlan G. & T.-P. To, 'The effect of fasting diets on medication management', *Medical Journal of Australia*, vol. 202, no. 3, pp. 131–32.

Malik, V.S. et al. (2010) 'Sugar-sweetened beverages and risk of metabolic syndrome and type 2 diabetes: a meta-analysis', *Diabetes Care*, vol. 33, no. 11, pp. 2477–83.

Martinez-Lapiscina E.H. et al. (2013) 'Mediterranean diet improves cognition: the PREDIMED-NAVARRA randomised trial', *Journal of Neurology, Neurosurgery and Psychiatry*, vol. 84, no. 12, pp. 1318–25.

Owen, R.W. et al. (2000) 'The antioxidant/anticancer potential of phenolic compounds isolated from olive oil', *European Journal of Cancer*, vol. 36, no. 10, pp. 1235–47.

Prentice, A.M. & S. A. Jebb (2003) 'Fast foods, energy density and obesity: a possible mechanistic link', *Obesity Reviews*, vol. 4, no. 4, pp. 187–94.

Ryan, M.C. et al. (2013) 'The Mediterranean diet improves hepatic steatosis and insulin sensitivity in individuals with non-alcoholic fatty liver disease', *Journal of Hepatology*, vol. 59, no. 1, pp. 138–43.

Sanchez-Villegas A. & M.A. Martinez-Gonzalez (2013) 'Diet, a new target to prevent depression?', *BMC Medicine*, vol. 11, no. 3, doi: 10.1186/1741-7015-11-3.

Sarri, K.O. et al. (2004) 'Greek Orthodox fasting rituals: a hidden characteristic of the Mediterranean diet of Crete', British Journal of Nutrition, vol. 92, no. 2, pp. 277–84.

Scheen, A.J. (2008) 'The future of obesity: new drugs versus lifestyle interventions', *Expert Opinion on Investigational Drugs*, vol. 17, no. 3, pp. 263–67.

Serra-Majem, L. et al. (2004) 'Mediterranean diet and health: is all the secret in olive oil?', *Pathophysiology of Haemostasis and Thrombosis*, vol. 33, no. 5–6, pp. 461–65.

Shai et al. (2008) 'Weight loss with a low-carbohydrate, Mediterranean or low-fat diet', *New England Journal of Medicine*, vol. 359, no. 3, pp. 229–41.

Shriner, R.L. (2013) 'Food addiction: detox and abstinence reinterpreted?', *Experimental Gerontology*, vol. 48, no. 10, pp. 1068–74.

Simopoulos, A.P. (2001) 'The Mediterranean diets: what is so special about the diet of Greece? The scientific evidence', *Journal of Nutrition*, vol. 131, no. 11, pp. 3065S–73S.

Simopoulos A.P. & L. Sidossis (2000) 'What is so special about the traditional diet of Greece: the scientific evidence', *World Review of Nutrition and Dietetics*, vol. 87, pp. 24–42.

Sofi, F. et al. (2011) 'Physical activity and risk of cognitive decline: a meta-analysis of prospective studies', *Journal of Internal Medicine*, vol. 269, no. 1, pp. 107–117.

Sofi, F. et al. (2010), 'Accruing evidence of benefits of adherence to the Mediterranean Diet on health: an update systemic review and meta-analysis. *American Journal of Clinical Nutrition*. vol. 39, no. 4, pp. 1189-96.

Sofi, F. et al, (2013), 'Mediterranean diet and health', *Biofactors*, vol 39, no. 4, pp. 335-42.

Su, Q. et al (2002) 'Identification and quantitation of major carotenoids in selected components of the Mediterranean diet: green leafy vegetables, figs and olive oil', *European Journal of Clinical Nutrition*, vol. 56, no. 11, pp. 1149–54.

Tapsell L.C. et al. (2006) 'Health benefits of herbs and spices: the past, the present, the future', *Medical Journal of Australia*, vol. 185, suppl. 4, pp. S4–S24.

Trepanowski, J.F. & R.J. Bloomer (2010) 'The impact of religious fasting on human health', *Nutrition Journal*, vol. 9:57.

Tressera-Rimbeau, A. et al. (2014) 'Polyphenol intake and mortality risk: a re-analysis of the PREDIMED trial', *BMC Medicine*, vol. 12: 77, doi:10.1186/1741-7015-12-77.

Trichopoulou, A. et al. (2014) 'Definitions and potential health benefits of the Mediterranean diet: views from experts around the world', *BMC Medicine*, vol. 12, pp. 112–29.

Trichopoulou A. et al. (2009) 'Anatomy of the health effects of the Mediterranean diet: Greek EPIC Prospective Cohort Study', *British Medical Journal*, vol. 338: b2337, www.bmj.com/content/338/bmj.b2337.

Trichopoulou, A. et al. (2003) 'Adherence to a Mediterranean diet and survival in a Greek population', *New England Journal of Medicine*, vol. 348, no. 26, pp. 2599–608.

Vasanti, S. et al. (2013) 'Sugar-sweetened beverages and weight gain in children and adults: a systematic review and meta-analysis', *Australian Journal of Clinical Nutrition*, vol. 98, no. 4, pp. 1084–102.

Vasto S. et al. (2014) 'Mediterranean diet and healthy ageing: a Sicilian perspective', *Gerontology*, vol. 60, no. 6, pp. 508–18.

Visioli, F. et al. (2005) 'Mediterranean food and health: building human evidence', *Journal of Physiology and Pharmacology*, vol. 56, suppl. 1, pp. 37–49.

Visioli, F. & C. Galli (2001) 'Antiatherogenic components of olive oil', *Current Atherosclerosis Reports*, vol. 3, no. 1, pp. 64–67.

Zuk, M. (2013) *Paleofantasy: What Evolution Really Tells Us about Sex, Diet, and How We Live*, W.W. Norton & Co., New York.

# ACKNOWLEDGEMENTS

This book is an extension of my previous book and could not have been developed without the tremendous support of my family, friends, colleagues and the Pan Macmillan team.

A dear friend Markos Dymiotis, a Cypriot migrant, who has spent decades cultivating an extensive Mediterranean fruit, vegetable and herbal garden in the suburbs of Melbourne, claims that the Greek Mediterranean grandmothers are 'the custodians of the traditional Greek cuisine'. Indeed they are of cuisine and many other cultural lifestyle practices.

In this book I have captured many family recipes from my mother Theano Itsiopoulos, my mother-in-law, Paraskevi Koutsis, my sister, Anna Itsiopoulos, cousin, Noula Karakonstantinou, and recipes from my dear friends and their mothers, Peter and Mary Amiridis, Helen Karikas, Con Barbounis, and my Italian friends, Rosy Calabro, and Franca Cincotti. Capturing these recipes was an enjoyable and interesting challenge which involved working alongside them and shoving (pushing) scales and measuring spoons in their path to get the ingredient quantities! Interpreting the method was another story!

A number of recipes in this book were inspired during a recent family trip to Europe where we visited Rome, Venice, Athens and Thessaloniki, and the Greek Islands (Lefkada, Zakynthos, Mykonos and Santorini) and I have many restauranteurs to thank for the wonderful dining experiences.

My gorgeous girls, Tiana and Vivienne Koutsis, embraced this project and contributed their own flair to the recipes and developed some of their own, and modernise some of mine! Tiana's love for the art of food and Vivienne's love and skill for cooking food fuelled (drove) me to complete this book and I hope they are both inspired to create their own memories through food.

My darling husband, Savvas Koutsis, has always been my inspiration in the kitchen with his love of food, fresh ingredients and entertaining friends with an abundance of food and wine of course. We spent many weekends together shopping at the Victoria Market for fresh ingredients to prepare the dishes in this book.

My research with the Mediterranean diet could not have been possible without my dear friend and colleague Professor Kerin O'Dea, who has mentored me for the past 20 years, and my friend and co-pilot through our PhD studies, Associate Professor Laima Brazionis, and I sincerely thank them for their review and contributions to this book and their ongoing influence in my career.

My dear friend of 30 plus years Associate Professor Antigone Kouris-Blazos, a Cretan descendant who has spent her career studying Greek migrants, has always encouraged the medicinal aspects of the traditional Mediterranean diet though her focus on herbs and spices.

We have built a large research team in the Mediterranean studies area at La Trobe University and collaborating universities and I would like to also acknowledge Dr Andrew Wilson, Dr Marno Ryan, Dr Audrey Tierney, Dr Colleen Thomas, Dr Mark Jois, Dr Jessica Radcliffe and our PhD students Tania Thodis, Speros Tsindos, Rachelle Opie, Elena Papamiltiadous, Teagan Kucianski and Hannah Mayr for their enthusiasm and commitment to our Mediterranean research program.

I would like to extend a very special thank you to the Pan Macmillan team for making this book possible. I thank Ingrid Ohlsson for her inspiration and mentorship, Samantha Sainsbury for her excellent management of the project which kept me on my toes, Nicola Young for her thorough and expert scientific editing, Caroline Velik for her wonderful creativity in food design, and John Laurie and his team for his talent with the lens which brought the recipes to life.

Finally, I would like to encourage the readers of this book to examine their own food cultures and capture the positive food experiences, from parents and grandparents and other significant people in their lives, and pass it on to the next generation.

## ABOUT THE AUTHOR

Associate Professor Catherine Itsiopoulos is the founding Head of Dietetics and Human Nutrition, and is the Department Head of Rehabilitation, Nutrition and Sport at La Trobe University. Her academic, clinical research, health service management and dietetics career spans 30 years and she is recognised for her expertise in studies using the Mediterranean diet in the treatment of diabetes, heart disease, obesity and fatty liver. Catherine leads a research program at La Trobe titled 'Food for Life' and has published widely in the scientific literature and presented her work nationally and internationally. Catherine's first cookbook titled *The Mediterranean Diet* (Pan Macmillan, 2013), focussed on research findings from her career and reviews of international evidence on the health benefits of the Mediterranean diet and includes traditional recipes from her research studies.

Catherine lives in Melbourne with her husband Savvas and daughters Tiana and Vivienne who all love to cook.